The 21st Century Christ-follower has many challenges that far exceed previous generations. It is on their shoulders we find ourselves standing so often. *Learning to Love the Master* not only allows you to stand on the shoulders of some faithful saints, it allows them to drape their arm behind your head and over your shoulders and to walk with you into the inner recesses of your soul. The inward journey disciples not only the head, but also the heart. It brings about the maturity of soul that Christians have, over the centuries, sought after. Anyone who meanders into their own heart will find the raging reckless love of Jesus, given by the Father, and personally applied by the Holy Spirit. Come join us friend. You'll never be the same.

– Matt Uldrich, D.Min., LPC, Missouri

Through *Learning to Love the Master* God has transformed our church. We've come to experience Christ's radical love and recognize his tender hand in our stories through the spiritual discipline of remembering. We've made the Retreat mandatory for our small groups and I highly recommend this material to anyone who wants to encounter Jesus in a fresh way.

– David Gainey, M.Div. Pastor, Oasis at Rita Ranch, Tucson, Arizona

My heart's desire is to see women get excited about Jesus and about discipleship. As a result of *Learning to Love the Master* being done by the women in our church I have been able to witness my heart's desire unfolding and blossoming.

– Kathy Creveston, past Director of Women's Ministries, Arizona

Learning to Love the Master came into my life at a time when I had been through some deep trials which had produced a hunger in me to know the Lord at a deeper level. This study proved to be just what I needed to fall more deeply in love with the Lord Jesus Christ and his Word. I stood in amazement not only for how He specifically spoke to me, but also that he brought a group of my friends

(continued)

and acquaintances together in a study group. Each woman spoke of how this came at just the right moment in their lives as well. For anyone ready and willing to look closely at his/her own life in relation to God's design and working, I highly recommend this study.

– Alice Forsythe Statler, retired missionary to Senegal, West Africa with WorldVenture

In *Pilgrim's Progress*, Christian embarks on a roadway to the Celestial City. The journey is not always what he expected and is filled with both joys and sorrows. He often loses his way until another comes along to help. Sometimes he is clearly aware of God's presence along the path and at other times - like Jacob in the wilderness - he only realizes later that the Lord was there all along. A.W. Tozer states that God is always "present, speaking, pleading, loving, working, and manifesting Himself whenever and wherever His people have the receptivity necessary to receive the manifestation." (*The Pursuit of God*)

I have found Patti Cepin and *Learning to Love the Master* to be God sent companions in discovering and re-discovering all the places along my way that God has been present - working, shaping, inviting and guarding. The insights have invited me into a fresh healing of my soul, enlarged my faith, given me a grander view of God's own story and have clarified the ongoing journey that God has shaped for me.

– Rev. Chris DeHaan, M.Div., Pastor, The Vineyard Christian Community, Tucson, Arizona

LEARNING TO LOVE THE MASTER

THE SPIRITUAL DISCIPLINE OF REMEMBERING:

A GUIDEBOOK

PATRICIA A. CEPIN

This is God's Word on the subject: "…I'll show up and take care of you as I promised and bring you back home. I know what I'm doing. I have it all planned out—plans to take care of you, not abandon you, plans to give you the future you hope for. When you call on me, when you come and pray to me, I'll listen. When you come looking for me, you'll find me. Yes, when you get serious about finding me and want it more than anything else, I'll make sure you won't be disappointed." God's Decree.

Jeremiah 29:10-13 (The Message)

JCM Press Tucson, Arizona

LEARNING TO LOVE THE MASTER, THE SPIRITUAL DISCIPLINE OF REMEMBERING: A GUIDEBOOK

For further information regarding spiritual formation experiences available through Journey Companion Ministries, go to www.journeycompanionsministries.org, call John Cepin at 520-795-8960 or email johncepin836@gmail.com.

Edited by Susan Cepin

ISBN: 978-0-9988036-0-9

Library of Congress Control Number: 2017904160

Printed in the United States of America

Second Printing: October, 2017

Contents

Learning to Love the Master was piloted in 1995. It was copyrighted into a formatted document in 1998 with a revised format in 2001. In 2008 it was revised and copyrighted into a retreat format. These previous formats were printed through Biblical Counseling Associates, Inc.

This 2017 copyright and revision is published by JCM Press, a publishing ministry of Journey Companions Ministries, Tucson, AZ 85712.

Acknowledgements

To all the men and women who have opened their lives to me and allowed me to peer into the heart of God: It brings tears to my eyes to even think of the impact you have had on me for the glory of God. Thank you from the bottom of my heart for trusting me with your stories.

To the twelve women who first allowed me to lead them on this uncharted journey where I held no map: thank you. I learned more in that year with you about God than I had in all the years prior.

Women of the "Burning Hearts," who took the risk to spend a concentrated time alone with God together on a mountaintop in Arizona writing our God Stories and sharing them with each other, weeping over His love for each of us—may you continue to reproduce after your own kind.

To the late Ruth Denler Meyers, whose tapes and Bible Studies taught my faltering heart to take its first steps toward a God who not only had a standard for my life but loved me enough to run me into the box canyon of Hosea 2:14—without your early journey, mine would not have been possible.

To Larry Crabb: You had the courage to love me by not listening to my demand that you let me please you. So much of who I am and who I have become is directly connected to the influence of your understanding of God and of man as he reflects God. You pushed me to think for myself in ways I never had, and then you told me to go out and teach others. This curriculum is the fruit of living into your exhortation. Thank you.

To the friends and co-laborers who read and reread and piloted some or all of this: your suggestions have been invaluable. This book would not exist without you. And to the many women and men who embraced this as your own and passed it on: Jesus is deeply blessed that you have facilitated Luke 13:34 for Him.

To Amy Malskite, untangler of my thoughts, like-minded woman of God—I love who God is in you. I love your growing courage to live from an unveiled face so that I can see Christ as He reveals Himself through you. I love what you do with my thoughts. Thanks for being willing to wade through the redundancies to get to the gold.

To our sons, Eric, Joel and Wesley, men who love God and people, who are as different as night and day from each other and yet who each live out their passion for Christ: Thank you for being God's 'iron sharpening iron' in my life—each of you from the day of your birth have been a gift that has made an indelible imprint on my soul. I could not be more proud. I watch in wonder as you continue your journey from one degree of glory to another. May Christ be praised!

To my three daughters I gained by way of my three sons: Susan, Blanca, and Laura, you are messages to me that God answers prayer and that He tailor-makes spouses—each of you is the perfectly unique help-meet for the man you married. Thank you for your obedience to God on their behalf. I love you.

To Susan Cepin, our first daughter and wife of Eric: How like God that thirty years into our relationship you would be the one to craft this into a compelling journey. Who else? You were thirteen when, with seven other teens, we began to think through how to know God deeply; see life's struggles through His eyes; and live out of both paradigms. In these pages, you have masterfully created form and direction out of the ofttimes random and 'run-on' portions of this work. You and Eric decided this needed to go to a larger audience, took all its random pieces, and handed me this finished work. We all know that left to myself this would not have happened. Dear word-crafter and kindred spirit, what a deep joy it is to co-labor with you and to see the labor of my life bear such beautiful fruit. You are that beautiful fruit and a gift to me.

To my husband, John: what a wild ride it has been! We started in the box canyon of Hosea 2:14 and have ended up on the high places running with hinds' feet. You are my best friend and the living example of the mercy and unconditional love of God to me. That has earned you many jewels. What a joy to know that when there is no back door to marriage, God can work miracles. Thanks for championing LLM and taking it to men. You have made it far more yours than mine, and God's heart rejoices to see you invite His warriors into conversation with Him. May the men you influence be as the sands on the seashore.

To Tim and Tammy Cahill, thank you for believing in this project. Your help has made this possible. Thanks for being our friends and co-laborers.

Last but not least, to my friend and a man after God's own heart, the late Edward Statler. You brought me the first rough draft of this work gleaned from many loose-leaf folders. You did so to take it back to the seminary you had founded in Senegal, West Africa to use as a course in mentoring. The rest is history. And to Alice, Ed's wife: You used this material with the women you poured your life into in ways I can only imagine. You even put it into French. You were one of the first twelve. That gives me goose bumps.

A Note From The Author

On the Cover is a painting by Greg Olsen of Jesus sitting on a hill above Jerusalem in the early light of dawn. I imagine His heart grieving as He cries,

> Jerusalem, Jerusalem, you who kill the prophets and stone those sent to you, how *often I have longed* to gather your children together, as a hen gathers her chicks under her wings, and you were not willing. (Luke 13:34, italics mine)

When I look at this picture, what comes to my mind is the Ancient of Days sitting on the mountain peaks of eternity, calling His children to Himself and grieving that we do not respond to Him. We are outside the Garden, living without that for which we were created, and steeped in a world full of evil. As He wept over His children in Jerusalem, Jesus was reflecting the heart of God grieving over our absence from the Garden. He grieves the fact that we are not walking in the Garden with Him even more than we do. We taste the grief in our souls but most often do not recognize its source. He identifies it clearly! He longs for us to long for His presence. He has always pursued those He loves: "The Lord appeared to us in the past, saying: 'I have loved you with an everlasting love; I have drawn you with unfailing kindness'" (Jeremiah 31:3). He continues to pursue His children with passion through each and every circumstance.

He invites you, now, to look for His footprints, for the touch of His hand, to listen for the rustle of the edges of His garments, the whisper of His voice. He invites you to look back and see His presence in your life in specific ways, perhaps in places you had not noticed before, places long forgotten. And you will begin to recognize Him in your present circumstances in new and precious ways. Our purpose here is to look into His eyes—to return His gaze and respond to the courtship of the living God.

Introduction

I would like to invite you on a journey. A pilgrimage, you might call it. Unlike travel into uncharted territories, this one will take you to familiar places. It is a pilgrimage into your past, where God has been actively, personally at work in ways perhaps previously hidden from your view. He has been drawing you to Himself through the years, shaping your experiences and inviting your heart to come alive to Him.

This journey began in 1995 when God asked me to develop a mentoring program for women at our church and to train the women to mentor. My intention was to condense what God had taught me during thirty-three years of mentoring and soul-care and teach a class to pass on what I had learned. God was quick to make it clear that this was not what He was asking me to do. He told me to interview interested women, and He would give me the map. What you have in your hands is what God gave us. He was telling each of us that we were to 'declare to others what we had seen and heard' of Him in our stories (1 John 1:3, author's paraphrase). He asked us to earnestly seek Him with the confidence that He would ignite our souls to cry with the Psalmist: "…my inner self thirsts for You, my flesh longs and is faint for You…. So I have looked upon You in the sanctuary to see Your power and Your glory" (Psalm 63:1-2, AMP).

As we dialogued weekly with God through our stories and shared them, our vision and understanding of God exploded. I wondered if it would be the same were we to use a retreat format to write our stories in a context of concentrated alone time. What a glorious time these retreats have been. Whether at a retreat center or 'camping out' at someone's home, God has showed up. What my heart learned about our God as I eavesdropped on countless conversations has transformed my intimacy with Him.

The husbands of these women began to ask why only women got to 'learn to love the Master,' so John began to gather groups of men together for weekend retreats. The solitude of the retreat format was very helpful in providing a space for the men to reflect. The men proved a safe and strong source of encouragement for each other as they listened to their unique God Stories unfold. As the men saw God's heart for them and where He had been present, their lives were often redirected and even transformed before their very eyes.

The purpose of *Learning to Love the Master* is to encourage Christ-followers at all stages of life and faith to find the fingerprints of the Master Potter on their lives where they have not had eyes to see them before. If you are new in your faith, it could be difficult to believe that God has been involved in your story before you bowed your knee to His Lordship. But this couldn't be further from the truth.

For those who have journeyed longer in their faith in Christ, *Learning to Love the Master* will help you not only to develop "eyes that see" God's movement in your life, but also to gain the courage to invite others on a journey with you to the feet of the Master. All too often, those who have been Christians for a significant period of time feel that they have nothing to offer. Or they feel that they do not know where to begin with a younger believer. However, each mature follower of Christ possesses a storehouse of rich experiences with the Master which they need only recognize to access. As you consider mentoring another in the faith, often your reluctance is because you may not be practicing in your own life the basic disciplines of the Christian life. The field guide will strengthen these disciplines in your own life and give you the confidence you will need to lead another in them.

You will encounter pain in this journey of remembering—pain that you may have tried to make sense of but haven't been able to, or pain that you have tried to ignore. God is waiting for you in these places, waiting to speak tenderly to you—if not the words you expect, yet the ones that your soul longs to hear.

So come with me, and let us remember what God has done! *Learning to Love the Master* is designed to put you in touch with where God has *already* been at work in your life and what He has *already* taught you. It is written to encourage you to walk with confidence in the identity He has uniquely given you, from which you can bless others. My prayer is that as you embark on this adventure, you will be overwhelmed by what He has taught you, by how much you discover that you already know about Him, and by how much you can actually invite others to share in your relationship with Him.

Holy Father, Lord Jesus, indwelling Holy Spirit, as we begin this journey, open our hearts to You. Open our eyes that we may see You more clearly. Invade our hearts that they might burn as did the hearts of the men on the road to Emmaus. We ask You to do exceeding abundantly above all we can think or ask, to Your glory and honor and to the furthering of Your Kingdom as You reveal the depth, height, length, and width of Your love.

Chapter 1
On Pilgrimage

Blessed (happy, fortunate, to be envied) is the man whose strength is in You, in whose heart are the highways to Zion. Passing through the Valley of Weeping (Baca), they make it a place of springs; the early rain also fills [the pools] with blessings. They go from strength to strength [increasing in victorious power]; each of them appears before God in Zion.
Psalm 84:5-7 AMP

HIGHWAYS TO ZION

God has been at work throughout your life, revealing Himself to you and teaching you the things you need to know in order to walk with Him. The aim of *Learning to Love the Master* is to reveal the highways to Zion which are hidden in your own heart. The journey to find and traverse these highways will be traveled in journal format. You will write your God Story, which is a narrative of how your life has intertwined with God's story. Through what events has He invited you to join Him? Where do you see His hand clearly evident in your life? What are the specifics? This process will bring into sharp focus what you have personally experienced of God.

As you rehearse for yourself, before the Lord, and before other believers what great things the Lord has done for you, you will grow in the confidence of knowing what, specifically, you possess to pass on to other believers who are younger in their faith. You may not know everything there is to know about a specific Christian discipline, but you will discover that you have some very concrete examples of the lessons God has taught you about Himself and His truths. You will be excited to share these truths with others.

This journey will pass through various stages: delving into the past, exploring the present, and considering God's direction for your future. Each passageway of this pilgrimage will require that you go to God and ask Him to reveal His presence to you: how He has interacted with you over the years, where He has shaped your experiences, what He has taught and is teaching you, and what He is calling you into. The most important aspect of these travels is one-on-one interaction with the Living God.

This is not an academic exercise but an excursion of the heart. This is not a Bible study—wonderful studies already abound—nor are we detailing a course to superimpose on somebody else. We are on a quest to discover our God and how we are each uniquely created in His image.

A Journey Of and Into Remembering

Each map reflects a history of people traveling through or dwelling in a specific geography. Likewise, as we take this particular pilgrimage into our own God Stories, we find ourselves in a spiritual context that is much larger than ourselves, a grand story that has been unfolding since the beginning of time. This story is woven together of the life narratives of many pilgrims—Abraham, Rahab, David, Abigail—and so many others whose names we won't know until we are united in worship before the throne of grace, at the feet of the King of Kings. These people struggled like we do—to find the presence of God in the ordinary and in the sometimes overwhelming confusion of life outside the garden. As you write your God Story, you will find Him where He has always been. You will find yourself a participant in a story that is much greater than you and your immediate context.

The Bible itself is a book of remembrance. It includes the God Stories of countless men and women. Notice how God says repeatedly, "Don't forget!" "Remember!" "Look back!" In fact, the word "remember" is repeated more than two hundred times throughout the Scriptures. Let's look at some of the passages that consider the importance of taking time to remember.

In the book of Exodus, we see how Moses' memories were written down both as a memorial and as an encouragement to Joshua. These men each faced different giants, but Joshua and others would draw strength from the legacy of God's faithfulness to Moses.

> Then the Lord said to Moses, "Write this on a scroll as something to be remembered and make sure that Joshua hears it, because I will completely blot out the name of Amalek from under heaven." (Exodus 17:14)

In Deuteronomy, the children of Israel were called to remember their time wandering around the Sinai Peninsula so that they might see God's involvement in and purpose for this chapter of their lives:

> Remember how the LORD your God led you all the way in the wilderness these forty years, to humble and test you in order to know what was in your heart, whether or not you would keep his commands. He humbled you, causing you to hunger and then feeding you with manna, which neither you nor your ancestors had known, to teach you that man does not live on bread alone but on every word

> that comes from the mouth of the LORD. (Deuteronomy 8:2-3)

When the children of Israel had finished crossing the Jordan River, the Lord instructed Joshua to lead the people in a tradition of remembering. This practice of establishing memorial stones would be found throughout the Old Testament in declaration of the miraculous works of God among His people:

> So Joshua called together the twelve men he had appointed from the Israelites, one from each tribe, and said to them, "Go over before the ark of the Lord your God into the middle of the Jordan. Each of you is to take up a stone on his shoulder, according to the number of the tribes of the Israelites, to serve as a sign among you. In the future, when your children ask you, 'What do these stones mean?' tell them that the flow of the Jordan was cut off before the ark of the covenant of the Lord. When it crossed the Jordan, the waters of the Jordan were cut off. These stones are to be a memorial to the people of Israel forever." … And Joshua set up at Gilgal the twelve stones they had taken out of the Jordan. He said to the Israelites, "In the future when your descendants ask their parents, 'What do these stones mean?' tell them, 'Israel crossed the Jordan on dry ground.'" (Joshua 4:4-7, 20-22)

In Psalm 77, David wrote:

> I remembered you, God, and I groaned; I meditated, and my spirit grew faint.… I thought about the former days, the years of long ago; I remembered my songs in the night. My heart meditated and my spirit asked.… Then I thought, "To this I will appeal: the years when the Most High stretched out his right hand. I will remember the deeds of the Lord; yes, I will remember your miracles of long ago. I will consider all your works and meditate on all your mighty deeds." Your ways, God, are holy. What god is as great as our God? …Your path led through the sea, your way through the mighty waters, though your footprints were not seen. You led your people like a flock by the hand of Moses and Aaron. (Psalm 77:3, 5-6, 10-13, 19-20)

And in Hebrews:

> Remember those earlier days after you had received the light, when you endured in a great conflict full of suffering. Sometimes you were publicly exposed to insult and persecution; at other times you stood side by side with those who were so treated. (Hebrews 10:32-33)

As we write our God Stories, we discover that the epic stories contained in

Scripture become our own in a new way. The loneliness and suffering that so many bore, the joy and hope that people have clung to for thousands of years, is the same that we find woven through our journeys. We are all part of the same story.

As we remember, our understanding will continue to deepen. Further, our God Stories not only excite us and bring great joy to our heavenly Father, but they also provide encouragement to others and create a bridge to the biblical narrative. In the future, when your descendants ask what God has done for you, you can tell them, "I will read my God Story to you; then you will see that He has done amazing things for me."

> My understanding of God's desire for us to remember came through doing word studies on the words *memory, memorial, remember, remembrance,* and *stone.* I invite you to explore these for yourself in the Scriptures. It is a rich study. One of the Hebrew words for remember is *zakar*, which also means "imprint." God wants to imprint what He has done for us on our minds and on our very hearts.

From Patti's God Story Journal

I will be sharing from my own God Story throughout this Guidebook for many reasons. The first is so you can see that this is a possible task. God does show up—and will—although not as we expect. I also hope that you will find new glimpses of God through my Story that you wouldn't have had otherwise and that in this you might have new access to your own narrative. You will find further excerpts from John and my God Stories in the Appendix. Be careful, though, that reading doesn't replace writing! Here is an excerpt from my God Story journal, written about a time before I bowed my knee to Jesus but during which I was already insatiably thirsty for God. In this and future excerpts from God Story journals, the voice of God is indicated by bold lettering.

Lord, remember when I was in nursing school and I would go to the chapel every morning to pray? It was You who put me in a Catholic school, wasn't it? Reminders of You were everywhere. You gave opportunities to debate with the nuns and priests over issues I didn't understand. Arguments with atheistic classmates just strengthened my resolve about who You were, Jesus, and the centrality of Your Person to the whole picture, even though I didn't know You personally at the time. That prayer of St. Francis of Assisi—You wanted me to find that and to begin to pray it for my own life. And I did, daily!

Yes, My child! I already knew what I had designed for you, and I was drawing you into that plan in very deliberate ways.

St. Francis' words are so clearly a picture of what You have given me to do with my life. That prayer is exactly what You are doing with my life today.

Prayer of Saint Francis of Assisi

Lord, make me an instrument of your peace.
Where there is hatred, let me sow love;
where there is injury, pardon;
where there is doubt, faith;
where there is despair, hope;
where there is darkness, light;
and where there is sadness, joy.
O Divine Master, grant that I may not so much seek
to be consoled as to console;
to be understood as to understand;
to be loved as to love.
For it is in giving that we receive;
it is in pardoning that we are pardoned;
and it is in dying that we are born to eternal life. Amen

Patti, listen to what I have asked you to pray. You will learn much about what I have planned for your life.
That whole year in the nursing program kept me searching for You. I see You ordering the pain and confusion of that year to drive me to You, and it worked.
Of course it did, child!
I had nowhere else to go. To whom could I turn, Lord? Only You have the words of life.

A Journey Of and Into Faith
The journey of remembering is a journey of faith. To listen to God, we must believe that He is speaking to us. To recognize His voice we must believe that He loves us, for His is the voice of love. However, we can also take tentative steps into conversation with the Almighty God and there discover anew His voice and the truth of His affection. This builds our faith as it leads us into a stronger confidence and intimacy with Him.

Pack the following biblical truths for your journey:

1) God loves you.
   The Lord appeared to us in the past, saying: "I have loved you with an everlasting love; I have drawn you with unfailing kindness." (Jeremiah 31:3)
2) Fellowship with the Triune God is a present reality, available to you.
   We proclaim to you what we have seen and heard, so that you also may have fellowship with us. And our fellowship is with the Father and with his Son, Jesus Christ. (1 John 1:3)
3) God cares about the details of your life.
   Record my misery; list my tears on your scroll—are they not in your record? (Psalm 56:8)
4) God's power and presence are greater than you know.
   And these are but the outer fringe of his works; how faint the whisper we hear of him! Who then can understand the thunder of his power? (Job 26:14)
5) God is not avoiding you, but wants to be sought out.
   "I revealed myself to those who did not ask for me; I was found by those who did not seek me. To a nation that did not call on my name,

I said, 'Here am I, here am I.'" (Isaiah 65:1)

6) God has initiated relationship with you; you need merely respond to Him.

    But God demonstrates his own love for us in this: While we were still sinners, Christ died for us. (Romans 5:8)

Allow these truths to provide a foundation as you take your first steps into new ways of interacting with God. Let them help you along your way.

A Journey Of and Into Intimacy

You will have opportunity during the course of this journey to engage with God's Word as the love letter that it is. That love letter, an intimate invitation from the God Who knows you, is calling you into deeper and greater intimacy with your Father.

Notice how God and Moses are described as communing and interacting directly:

> And the Lord spoke to Moses face to face, as a man speaks to his friend. Moses returned to the camp, but his minister Joshua son of Nun, a young man, did not depart from the [temporary prayer] tent. Moses said to the Lord, See, You say to me, Bring up this people, but You have not let me know whom You will send with me. Yet You said, I know you by name and you have also found favor in My sight. Now therefore, I pray You, if I have found favor in Your sight, show me now Your way, that I may know You [progressively become more deeply and intimately acquainted with You, perceiving and recognizing and understanding more strongly and clearly] and that I may find favor in Your sight. And [Lord, do] consider that this nation is Your people. And the Lord said, My Presence shall go with you, and I will give you rest. And Moses said to the Lord, If Your Presence does not go with me, do not carry us up from here! … And the Lord said to Moses, I will do this thing also that you have asked, for you have found favor, loving-kindness, and mercy in My sight and I know you personally and by name. (Exodus 33:11-15, 17 AMP)

This same fellowship is available to us through Jesus Christ:

> You are my friends if you do what I command. I no longer call you servants, because a servant does not know his master's business. Instead, I have called you friends, for everything that I learned from my Father I have made known to you. (John 15:14-15)

In the Song of Songs, we see the beloved respond as one who has caught a glimpse of God's heart:

> My beloved speaks and says to me, Rise up, my love, my fair one, and come away…. [So I went with him, and when we were climbing the rocky steps up the hillside, my beloved shepherd said to me] O my dove, [while you are here] in the seclusion of the clefts in the solid rock, in the sheltered and secret place of the cliff, let me see your face, let me hear your voice; for your voice is sweet, and your face is lovely. [My heart was touched and I fervently sang to him my desire]. (Song of Solomon 2:10, 14-15 AMP)

Hosea presents a beautiful word picture of this reality:

> Yet I taught Ephraim to walk, taking them by their arms or taking them up in my arms, but they did not know that I healed them. I drew them with cords of a man, with bands of love, and I was to them as one who lifts up and eases the yoke over their cheeks, and I bent down to them and gently laid food before them. (Hosea 11:3-4 AMP)

Listen to the painful cry of God's heart as He considers the waywardness of the ones He so deeply loves:

> How can I give you up, O Ephraim! How can I surrender and cast you off, O Israel! How can I make you as Admah or how can I treat you as Zeboiim [both destroyed with Sodom]! My heart recoils within Me; My compassions are kindled together. (Hosea 11:8 AMP)

Come to the feet of Jesus. See just how precious you are to Him. Enter the love affair of your life with renewed passion and single-mindedness. Hosea 2:14 says, "Therefore I am now going to allure her; I will lead her into the wilderness and speak tenderly to her." Are you willing to believe that these words could be spoken of you? God has done these very things every day of your life; you have often missed the details in the busyness of the moment. He is inviting you to stop, look back, listen, and be amazed. We fear encountering our own souls, but true freedom can only come when we choose to sit alone in conversation with Him about the formation of His Glory in us.

> As I counsel victims of abuse, I am often stunned by the way they come alive even more than others as they discover God's love. Even though they have often deadened their souls to cope with a history of severe pain and damage, God's light and healing can bring radical transformation. The deeper your need to know the love of the Lord Jesus Christ, the deeper your experience of coming alive with joy in Him will be. He never ceases to amaze me with His gentle pursuit of our hearts. Praise Him! The enemy will not win.

My husband and I often reminisce about the early days of our relationship and the feelings and thoughts we had about one another. Always there is a drawing back into those early emotions, when we were so caught up in the newness of what we had together. We come away from those times feeling both loved and more loving. As you begin to reflect on your romance with God, let this time kindle your passion for Him. Look at the particulars—the tenderness, the little signs of His presence—of how He first loved you and how He continues to love you! His desire is that we adore Him and experience His passion for us. This God we serve is neither distant nor disinterested.

A Journey Of and Into Community

As you can see, our stories are woven of the same threads as those who preceded us on the path toward God. While we don't have a conversational connection with these brothers and sisters, yet they form a part of our community of faith. Speaking of these predecessors, Hebrews 12:1-2 says, "Therefore, since we are surrounded by such a great cloud of witnesses, let us throw off everything that hinders and the sin that so easily entangles. And let us run with perseverance the race marked out for us, fixing our eyes on Jesus, the pioneer and perfecter of faith."

A primary purpose of this Guidebook is to help equip Christians to mentor other believers. This assumes that the reader is already contextualized in a faith community in which truth is being taught and practiced. Whether or not this is the case for you, there has been someone who passed the torch of faith to you, either directly or indirectly. And there will be others to whom God invites you to extend the gospel. We see in 1 John 1:3 that fellowship with the triune God creates a call to deep Christian community: "We proclaim to you what we have seen and heard, so that you also may have fellowship with us. And our fellowship is with the Father and with his Son, Jesus Christ."

You will have opportunity along this journey to consider your own personal relationships, both past and present. But if you choose to embark on the pilgrimage as herein described, you will also travel with a group of committed companions, referred to as your cohort. This Guidebook can be valuable whether used individually or in a group setting, but the power of its use in a group cannot be overstated. Our stories were meant to be shared and heard, and we often see God yet more clearly as we tell our stories to others and listen to theirs.

Shared conversation engages each of our hearts with the way God loves the person reading, and we hear our story in theirs in ways we did not know were possible. Just as He uses each thing put at His disposal to access your heart and communicate His presence, so His presence in your story will resonate with others. The sound that has burned within your heart burns in the hearts of your fellow sojourners as you invite them into your revelation—the conversation where God has revealed to you where He was and what He was doing.

Consider the powerful fellowship that John witnessed and experienced as he led a cohort of men on a *Learning to Love the Master* weekend retreat:

> I was not prepared for what God did that weekend and what He has continued to do each time a group of men take the time to enter conversation with Him about their stories. We have found true what Paul wrote to the church at Corinth, that no eye has seen, no ear has heard, no mind has conceived what God has prepared for those who love Him (1 Corinthians 2:9). But God has revealed it to us by His Spirit, and so we met God, both in our own stories and in the story of every man who joined us. As we took time to read to each other from our stories—what we have remembered, seen and heard—it was like we had been invited to eavesdrop. We were captured by the intimate love of this God who has woven us in our mother's womb for His purposes, His glory and His pleasure. We knew that He takes pleasure in His sons, but together we experienced Him taking pleasure in us. We asked for a new way of knowing Him, and He showed us the specifics of His love in our stories. We listened to one another's conversations and were brought into His Presence in ineffable ways. His relentless pursuit of each man through his life brought new levels of clarity to the call of God on each of our lives.

Our responses to God were as unique as the individual men who participated. One man was so moved by finding God in his story that he led his family in writing and sharing their stories with each other. This family was deeply touched by God and drawn to each other as a result. Over and over I am amazed at how much you come to love another person when you see how much God loves them. During the weekend there were times when the presence of the Holy Spirit had some among us prostrate on the floor, crying out to God for repentance and forgiveness of our sins. In the light of God's love, not only our lives but our sins took on a different hue. As we left the retreat together, we agreed that because of this time, none of us would be the same. There have been times when we have been called on by God to draw our Swords of Truth and fight against the darkness for the heart of one among us. Often our times with God are deeply emotional; each time we hear the Voice of God speaking clearly in a man's story, our hearts burn at the sound of His Voice.

These times of conversing with God and sharing our stories with other men prepare us to renew our allegiance to Jesus and the coming of His Kingdom here on earth. It also deepens our call to fight against the darkness that surrounds people held captive by the enemy's lies. We have not been called as men to scale mountains and jump off cliffs as much as we have been called to stand against the darkness, against the rulers of spiritual darkness in high places.

I have learned that our weapons are honed nowhere other than at the feet of Jesus, where we gain strength to fight. He is our great example; His time alone with God gave Him strength to do not His own will, but the will of the Father. He allowed the Father to interpret His story for Him. In this freedom, He was able to live out of who He really was, not just who the world wanted Him to be. We must do the same; but in order for us to love the Master more deeply, we need to learn in new ways how much we are loved by Him. We must be men who can say, "I have finished what The Father has called me to do." We can only say that if we have spent much time at the feet of Jesus.

LOCATING YOURSELF ON THE MAP

Take a few moments to reflect on this chapter and assess your current whereabouts:

- *Looking back on your life, what indications do you have that God has been present with you all along?*
- *When you consider your earlier memories, do you sense God's activity in your life?*
- *What would you say is the current state of your faith?*
- *How have you become aware that God is inviting you into deeper intimacy with Himself?*
- *How would you describe the role of Christian community in your life now? Previously?*

Chapter 2
Field Guide

**Then those who feared the Lord talked often one to another;
and the Lord listened and heard it, and a book of remembrance was written before Him
of those who reverenced and worshipfully feared the Lord and who thought on His name.
Malachi 3:16 AMP**

ITINERARY

Let's get started! Whether you are striking out with a group or undertaking a solo expedition, your trip begins with *Daily Devotional Journaling*, as described later in this chapter. **Start into this right away**. Begin to incorporate the Disciplines explained below as you read through Chapters 3, 4, and 5. Chapter 6 will bring you to the *Progressions*, where you will begin writing your God Story even as you continue to practice Daily Devotional Journaling and Scripture memory. Take your time with these interactive writing assignments. When you finish one Progression, read the next section, which will in turn introduce another Progression. Pursue evidences of God's presence as you pass through each segment of this pilgrimage. Record what He shows you.

This Guidebook incorporates specific instruction for the use of *Learning to Love the Master* in a group format for the purpose of developing Christian mentors. Those interested in leading such a group will find Chapter 12 particularly useful. However, Chapter 12 also explains how to utilize the contents of this Guidebook to accommodate a modified group (see *On Shorter Trips and Limited Expeditions*) or to facilitate a weekend retreat (see *On Running a Learning to Love the Master Retreat*).

The Cohort

If you are undertaking this pilgrimage in a group setting, your group of fellow sojourners will be herein referred to as your cohort. You will meet with your cohort on a regular basis to pray together and listen to each other's written journeys. In order for the group to function at its best, you must honor each person and the content of his or her writing. Please commit to the following together:

Cohort Promise

I will maintain in strictest confidence all that is said in the group by others. I will only discuss myself or the person from the group to whom I am speaking.

I will not discuss a third member of the group with another member. I may, however, discuss what I am learning and the content of my own journals with anyone I choose. I will not allow any offense, either toward me or from me within this cohort to go unreconciled. At the earliest possible moment, I will offer grace to my brother/sister in the group.

Journey Companion
Your Journey Companion is the accountability partner from your cohort with whom you will pray 30 minutes a week. You will also listen to each other's verses each week and help each other to succeed with the goals of this journey in whatever way possible, encouraging one another to be faithful to Devotional Journaling and the process of writing the God Story journal. This may be difficult, but will bear lasting fruit. Some have found that the easiest way to accomplish this task is by meeting 30-45 minutes before the regularly scheduled group sessions.

THE DISCIPLINES
Following, you will find instructions on aspects of this pilgrimage designed to sharpen the Christian disciplines in your life:

1. **Scripture Memory**
   Scripture memory provides a lasting foundation which is readily available at any time for use by the Holy Spirit. The Topical Memory System, published by the Navigators, provides a method for memorizing and review which can build discipline and aid in a lasting grasp of memorized passages. I particularly like this system because it teaches good skills for future success in memorization. This will give you an effective tool for your own life and a systematic way to equip young believers to master the Sword of the Spirit.

> Of all the tools for spiritual growth in my life, Scripture memory has been the most powerful. The Word of God washes over my mind and transforms my thinking. When I have strayed, the Holy Spirit has used the Word hidden in my heart to convict me and bring me back. Memorized Scripture provides the backbone of my soul-care ministry as well.

2. **Year Verse**
   A friend once shared with me the value of choosing a special verse for my life

each New Year. The verse was either one I felt I needed or one that God had seemed to bring to my attention as I read. One year I chose Ephesians 4:1-2. These verses speak of walking "in a manner worthy of the calling with which you have been called, with all humility and gentleness, with patience, showing forbearance to one another in love" (NASB). I memorized these verses and began to study them. What is my calling? What is humility and forbearance? How could I begin to practice these qualities? I placed the verses over the sink and kept them on a card in my Bible. I meditated on those verses and prayed that God would give me understanding of my specific calling and that my life would begin to evidence humility, patience, and gentleness. In the years that followed, I have continued to ask God for a verse each year that He wants to use in shaping and directing me.

D. L. Moody said, "The Scriptures were not given to increase our knowledge, but to change our lives." I encourage you to choose a verse for this year. Ask God to use it to change your life.

3. **Life Verse**

Early in my Christian life someone suggested that I ask God to give me a verse for my life, a verse expressing the desire God had for the direction that my life would take for Him. After prayerful consideration, I believe God gave me the following verse: "I want to know Christ—yes, to know the power of his resurrection and participation in his sufferings, becoming like him in his death" (Philippians 3:10).

I began to pray that this verse would be true for my life, and I began to filter my life through its truths. Two and a half years later, as I was seeking God's will regarding a sixteen-month mission trip with Operation Mobilization, God gave me Isaiah 58. That chapter has become my life *chapter*, reflecting my life goals and directions. I refer to it often for further insight, conviction of sin, and confirmation of life choices.

Recently, I have seen how often God takes me back to the book of Hosea, and I am beginning to consider the possibility that He is telling me it is my life *book*. God has spent many years teaching me about my heart and His from this book. The desert of Hosea 2:14 is a place where He and I often meet.

Begin to ask God to give you a verse, a passage, a chapter, or even a whole book of the Bible for your life. You will want to share these verses, as well as your year verse(s), with your Journey Companion and your whole cohort for the purpose of praying wisely for one another.

DEVOTIONAL JOURNALING

Devotional Journaling is both preparation for the journey of *Learning to Love the Master* and nourishment for the days to come. It provides a rhythm for a life spent communing with God.

You will need:

1) Your own personal devotional journal.
2) A Bible in the translation of your choice—in book form, not digital, so that you can mark the pages.
3) While not essential, a Bible reading plan can be helpful to direct your reading.

Choose a specific book of the Bible to begin reading consecutively and consistently on a daily basis. Begin at the start of that book and do not move on to another book of Scripture until you have completed it. Place your focus each day, however, not on the amount of reading you do, but on the quality of your interaction with God.

As you read, mark what stands out to you. Afterwards, review what you have marked; select the idea that stands out most. Write out the verse(s) containing this thought. Journal what God is saying to you about this passage and record your response to Him. Write in first person, from yourself ("I") to God ("You"). Write what God is saying to you in first person as well, from Himself ("I") to you (using your name when applicable). Delineate God's words to you by placing them in quotes or writing them in a different color of ink. You may also use quotes or a specific color of ink to designate words straight from Scripture. This is an interactive process: read His Word, listen to His voice, and respond in writing. Avoid writing a list of prayer requests. Focus instead on having a written conversation with God.

Your Devotional Journal will become a record of your ongoing conversations with God. While many of these dialogues will be rooted in Scripture reading, your journal entries may take on a variety of other forms. You may ask a question and record the answer you hear from your heavenly Father. Or you might write out a running dialogue about an area in life you are wrestling with. God's words to you may come directly through the Scriptures, or He may communicate with you through a book you are reading, a conversation with a friend, or words whispered by the Holy Spirit as you move through your day.

The beauty of the devotional journaling process is that it establishes an ongoing record of what God is saying to you and doing in your life. Devotional journaling will build your confidence as it reveals patterns of God's plan for your life, giving you *eyes that see*, and over time provides a sense of your full heritage in the Lord.

As you look back over time, you will be able to recognize consistent messages, themes, and direction that your Father is communicating to you.

> As I began working on this Guidebook for *Learning to Love the Master*, I went back to my Devotional Journal and saw how God had been preparing me the entire previous year to move in this direction. I saw how He was answering my cries for people who desired to mentor others from their own experience with Him.

"The faintest ink is better than the clearest memory." - Chinese proverb

Devotional Journaling:

- Helps us to become intentional in our relationships with God
- Makes God's direction for our lives clear
- Supports reading the Bible in a way that is interactive and personal
- Keeps us on track in our Bible reading
- Gives us accountability to the daily discipline of Bible reading
- Provides a book of remembrance

Let me share a conversation with God which I recorded as a journal entry during a *Learning to Love the Master* retreat with a group of young mothers, regarding what was on my heart for them. It originated from my reading of Romans 1:

> …Every time I think of you in my prayers, which is practically all the time, I ask him to clear the way for me to come and see you. The longer this waiting goes on, the deeper the ache. I so want to be there to deliver God's gift in person and watch you grow stronger right before my eyes! (Romans 1:9-11 The Message)

> I so understand Paul's heart here. This weekend being in my heart has been a curious journey for me. A deep sadness has been with me. Not depression, but sorrow for the 'not yet' and sorrow that I will not be the one to pour my life into these young women or be around them to watch You work. I know You are offering me something new about Your heart, something of Your longing for these young women. What has it been like for You to have limited Yourself the way You have?

Patti, I have often longed to gather them around Me as a mother hen gathers her chicks around her.
That longing is akin to the jealousy You felt with regard to the Israelites; You are jealous for their presence.
Yes child, it is. I grieve for the ones that will not come when I call them. I have removed the great barrier, but all is not yet well. I am anticipating being face to face with them so that they can know it is Me who has been there all along.
Open my heart to Your heart, Lord. You are jealous for Your children; jealousy hurts. Lord Jesus, I hear that You are longing to have them come and sit at Your feet as Mary did. I will speak that invitation for You – I will gather them to You. I will lend my arms, my voice, and my feet.
You have heard My heart, child.

SETTING OUT

As a first step into the process of Devotional Journaling, you will read Psalm 139 and write interactively about it, recording both your thoughts toward God and what you hear Him saying to you. If you are journeying with a cohort, this first writing exercise will be done together in a group session. Consider this a guided practice run for your future daily Devotional Journaling.

Psalm 139 is an anchor for your faith. It explores the wonderful reality that God has been present with you from your mother's womb, unraveling the particulars of where and how. God has relentlessly pursued you from the day of your birth. He hovered over you when you had no idea He was there. You were *created* to enjoy relationship and impact! You may return to this Psalm later, either as a place to begin writing your God Story or further in as a way to get ideas flowing should you get stuck.

Before you begin, ask God to deepen—or awaken—a thirst in you to find Him as more of who He really is, not just as you have known Him already. As David wrote in Psalm 42: "As a deer pants for water, so my soul pants for thee."

Let's ask some questions of God and reflect as we read through the Psalm. Feel free to jot down your own questions and thoughts next to the ones already listed. In your Devotional Journal, write down questions as you ask them of God. Then wait and listen for His answers. Write these down, along with further questions and replies that arise. Record your own reflections and responses to God as well.

PSALM 139 MEDITATION
(Psalm 139 AMP)

Vs 1 - O Lord, You have searched me [thoroughly] and have known me.
What have You found there that delights You Abba?

Vs 2 - You know my downsitting and my uprising; You understand my thought afar off.
Lord, did You sit down with me when I sat down? What were You doing while we were sitting there? Were You speaking to me? What were You saying?

Vs 3-4 - You sift and search out my path and my lying down, and You are acquainted with all my ways. For there is not a word in my tongue [still unuttered], but, behold, O Lord, You know it altogether.
Abba, nothing about me is a secret to You, and still You are committed to forming Christ in me and using me. That is so amazing to me. Why would You want to be acquainted with all my ways? Help me understand the significance of that to my daily life, both then and now. Show me Yourself in those places.

Vs 5-6 - You have beset me and shut me in—behind and before, and You have laid Your hand upon me. Your [infinite] knowledge is too wonderful for me; it is high above me, I cannot reach it.
Really, You actually reach out and put Your hand on me? When, Lord? Show me those times; take me back to the places in my life where You reached out and covered me with Your hand.

Vs 7 - Where could I go from Your Spirit? Or where could I flee from Your presence? *Abba, You are never absent, are You? Nor have You ever been, though there are times I wish You had not been there, times of so much shame. What were You doing in those times when I grieved Your Great Heart with my sin? You gave me this chapter because You knew I would need to know that You have stayed with me through all the ups and downs in my life. Thank You, Abba.*

Vs 9-10 - If I take the wings of the morning or dwell in the uttermost parts of the sea, even there shall Your hand lead me, and Your right hand shall hold me.

Just like You were with Ephraim in Hosea 11 – You stooped down to feed me, You carried me in Your arms, even when I did not know it. Abba, where specifically were You doing this in my life?

Vs 11-12 - If I say, Surely the darkness shall cover me and the night shall be [the only] light about me, even the darkness hides nothing from You, but the night shines as the day; the darkness and the light are both alike to You.
It is clear that I have not been able to hide from You. There are no secrets. Your very Presence drives darkness away. And Abba, how many times have You rescued me from unknown danger, and from known danger? Show me those times to deepen my understanding of Your continual care. Are You offering me grace for the future in these verses as well Abba?

Vs. 13 - You did form my inward parts; You did knit me together in my mother's womb. *Form and knit – those are not passive words. You chose the colors of the yarn, the genes – I am created exactly as You wished.*

Vs 14 - I will confess and praise You for You are fearful and wonderful and for the awful wonder of my birth! Wonderful are Your works, and that my inner self knows right well.
How can my heart not swell with praise when I think of the implications of Your Presence during the period of my gestation and at my delivery? I have been loved and safe – even when circumstances seemed the opposite.

Vs 15 - My frame was not hidden from You when I was being formed in secret [and] intricately and curiously wrought [as if embroidered with various colors] in the depths of the earth [a region of darkness and mystery].
There are those colors, You chose my colors; bring light to those colors as they developed in my childhood. Show me the Life Message You wove into my being from the very beginning.

Vs 16 - Your eyes saw my unformed substance, and in Your book all the days [of my life] were written before ever they took shape, when as yet there was none of them.
As Ephesians 2:10 says, You designed and planned my days with a purpose in mind.

Vs 17 - How precious and weighty also are Your thoughts to me, O God! How vast is the sum of them!
Abba, teach me to be a collector of Your thoughts toward me.

Vs 18 - If I could count them, they would be more in number than the sand. When I awoke, [could I count to the end] I would still be with You.
As I seek Your face to hear the specifics of Your thoughts to me down through my life, truly they are precious. I look forward to reading Your Love Letters all over again. Rekindle my first love, Abba.

Vs 19-20 - If You would [only] slay the wicked, O God, and the men of blood depart from me - who speak against You wickedly, Your enemies who take Your name in vain!
Lord, it breaks my heart the way the wicked blaspheme You, the way they misuse Your name.

Vs 21-22 - Do I not hate them, O Lord, who hate You? And am I not grieved and do I not loathe those who rise up against You? I hate them with perfect hatred; they have become my enemies.
I am on Your side against those who hate You, those who oppose You. Your enemies are my enemies. Lord those are hard words to say. But as I hate the way they dishonor and disregard You, at the same time I can follow Jesus' counsel to show love to and pray for those who are spiteful toward You. What an amazing act. Thank You for this gift which keeps my heart soft and free from bitterness.

Vs 23-24 - Search me [thoroughly], O God, and know my heart! Try me and know my thoughts! And see if there is any wicked or hurtful way in me, and lead me in the way everlasting.
Lord, I am aware that You search and know my heart. You know my anxious, troubled thoughts and then test me to reveal them to me before I speak them. You are quick to point out anything in me that offends You. My prayer is that the floodlight of Your Word and Your Spirit will keep my feet on the path of never unwittingly joining your enemies. Thank You for all the times You have searched my heart and exposed what You have found there. Thank You for granting me repentance.

Chapter 3
The Pain

[For my determined purpose is] that I may know Him [that I may progressively become more deeply and intimately acquainted with Him, perceiving and recognizing and understanding the wonders of His Person more strongly and more clearly], and that I may in that same way come to know the power outflowing from His resurrection [which it exerts over believers], and that I may so share His sufferings as to be continually transformed [in spirit into His likeness even] to His death.
Philippians 3:10 AMP

ENCOUNTERING PAIN ALONG YOUR JOURNEY

As you journal through your life, you may well encounter painful memories that you did not expect. Some of these memories may be familiar but have been carefully avoided. Others may emerge as new to you. Let me invite you to journey with me toward God's perspective on pain.

Pain is a reality for those of us living outside the Garden of Eden. Keep in mind that it is not just fallen creation that experiences pain. The heart of God is in pain, because outside of the Garden we no longer walk with Him face to face. God grieves that we are living in the presence of sin in a world governed by Satan. We are not *of* this world, but we *are* in it. However, our God is a redeeming God. He not only rescues our souls from destruction, but He buys back the painful situations of our lives for His purposes of healing and good.

Unfortunately, instead of turning to our Father for redemption, we often choose to trust in our own abilities, or what Jeremiah called "the arm of the flesh" (Jeremiah 17:5-8). The consequence of making our lives work apart from God is that to do so blinds us to the good. When God's goodness arrives on the scene, we are unable to recognize it, because it doesn't match up with our expectations. The path out of this dark place is to accept God's invitation to trust *Him* rather than our own abilities or perceptions. He is inviting us to walk into the Refiner's fire. Here, He promises to meet us. In Isaiah 43, He promises, "When you pass through the waters, I will be with you.... When you walk through the fire, you will not be burned" (Isaiah 43:2). He meets us in the difficult places.

Since God is sovereign and good: if there is pain in our lives, He intends to use it for our good. If God meets us in our pain, then the pain itself is not the problem. Rather, the problem is our demand that we not experience pain. Don't get me wrong—sin *is* at the root of all pain: we experience pain because of other people's sin against us, our sin against others, and the general abundance of sin in this fallen world. Yes, sin causes pain. But our loving God has allowed us to experience this pain. He has not removed the consequences of the Fall. Our response is to demand relief. We are unwilling to sit in the pain He has allowed. We work frantically to make it go away, because the voices clamoring at us from all sides tell us that we should not be in pain.

C.S. Lewis called pain God's "megaphone to rouse a deaf world." Indeed, it is an invitation to which we must respond. Our heavenly Father uses pain for a variety of purposes. While pain comes from many directions into our lives, *always* the hand of our Father directs it in His love for us.

Pain's Schoolroom

Pain teaches many lessons. To list only a few:

- Pain brings me into a deeper understanding of God.

  My ears had heard of you but now my eyes have seen you. (Job 42:5)
- Pain requires that I be dependent on and connected to God.

  Therefore, in order to keep me from becoming conceited, it was given me a thorn in my flesh, a messenger of Satan, to torment me. Three times I pleaded with the Lord to take it away from me. But he said to me, "My grace is sufficient for you, for my power is made perfect in weakness." Therefore I will boast all the more gladly about my weaknesses, so that Christ's power may rest on me. That is why, for Christ's sake, I delight in weaknesses, in insults, in hardships, in persecutions, in difficulties. For when I am weak, then I am strong. (2 Corinthians 12:7-10)
- Pain enables me to comfort others with the comfort God brings to me.

  Praise be to the God and Father of our Lord Jesus Christ, the Father of compassion and the God of all comfort, who comforts us in all our troubles, so that we can comfort those in any trouble with the comfort we ourselves receive from God. (2 Corinthians 1:3-4)
- Pain perfects and completes me.

  Consider it pure joy, my brothers and sisters, whenever you face trials of many kinds, because you know that the testing of your faith produces perseverance. Let perseverance finish its work so that you may be mature and complete, not lacking anything. (James 1:2-4)

- Pain brings me to repentance.

  Godly sorrow brings repentance that leads to salvation and leaves no regret, but worldly sorrow brings death. See what this godly sorrow has produced in you: what earnestness, what eagerness to clear yourselves, what indignation, what alarm, what longing, what concern, what readiness to see justice done. At every point you have proved yourselves to be innocent in this matter. (2 Corinthians 7:10-11)

- Pain draws me into His arms where I find the intimacy with Him my heart was created to enjoy.

  Come, let us return to the Lord. He has torn us to pieces but he will heal us; he has injured us but he will bind up our wounds. After two days he will revive us; on the third day he will restore us, that we may live in his presence. (Hosea 6:1-2)

- Pain accomplishes God's purposes for good.

  You intended to harm me, but God intended it for good to accomplish what is now being done, the saving of many lives. (Genesis 50:20)

- Pain produces an eternal weight of glory far beyond all comparison.

  Therefore we do not lose heart. Though outwardly we are wasting away, yet inwardly we are being renewed day by day. For our light and momentary troubles are achieving for us an eternal glory that far outweighs them all. So we fix our eyes not on what is seen, but on what is unseen, since what is seen is temporary, but what is unseen is eternal. (2 Corinthians 4:16-18)

A World Without Pain

Think about the consequences of living in a world in which there was no physical pain. Like a person with leprosy, if a rat were to bite my toe, what would happen? I would not feel it, and infection may set in. Likewise, what would be the product of a fallen world which offered no personal pain? What would happen if God removed the consequences of all sin? The Israelites give us a glimpse of the possible results when they offer their children as burnt sacrifices to the false god Molech (2 Kings 23:10). The wickedness of mankind would have no end.

We see in Hosea 2:6-20 how God uses pain for good. God allows pain in the life of Israel, His chosen people, likened here to a faithless wife. Instead of thirsting for God in the way of the Psalmist, she is off like a woman searching for her many lovers. None of her strategies to independently acquire her longings succeed. God hedges her in. But instead of speaking to her in anger, He says, 'Therefore, behold, I will allure you, I will bring you into the wilderness, alone and apart, and I will speak kindly, tenderly, to your heart' (Hosea 2:14, author's paraphrase). Once God has His beloved's attention, He gives from *His* hand all she has sought from her other lovers.

Have you ever realized the pains to which the Lover of your soul has gone to get your attention? He loves you with an everlasting love; He has created you as His portion. He stoops down with all the love of a nursing mother. With all the passion of first love, He draws you to Himself. He wants you to know how He feels about you. Dan Allender has said that "it is *in* the Valley of the Shadow of Death that He sets a table before us and He gently treats our wounds." We *will* be wounded, we *will* walk in that dark valley, but He is there, waiting for us. Only those with the courage to go with Him into the valley will know the secret of His presence.

THE FELLOWSHIP OF HIS SUFFERING

There is another aspect of pain that I have just begun to wrap my heart, mind, and soul around. I speak as a fellow sojourner who continues to discover the fellowship with God that comes from the experience of suffering. Come with me as we explore.

This door opened to me when I was counseling a couple in a week-long, intensive format. One morning in my time alone with Jesus I was struck by the words used about Him in His Gethsemane experience. Luke 22:44 describes Him as "being in *agony* of mind" (AMP, italics mine). Matthew says, "He began to show *grief* and *distress of mind* and was *deeply depressed.* Then He said to them, 'My soul is *very sad* and *deeply grieved*, so that I am almost *dying of sorrow*'" (Matthew 26:37-38 AMP, italics mine). Mark says He was "*struck with terror and amazement*" and "*deeply troubled.*" The King James Version renders this as, "'My soul is *exceeding sorrowful*, even unto death....'"

As we counseled that morning we were struck with how much God was using my clients' pain for good. The pain was drawing them into fellowship with God. I was at once reminded of Philippians 3:10:

> [For my determined purpose is] that I may know Him [that I may progressively become more deeply and intimately acquainted with Him, perceiving and recognizing and understanding the wonders of His Person more strongly and more clearly], and that I may in that same way come to know the power outflowing from His resurrection [which it exerts over believers], and that I may so share His sufferings as to be continually transformed [in spirit into His likeness even] to His death. (AMP)

How quickly I had slipped by those words in the past. This is my life verse! How could I have missed the significance of those words, "that I may know Him… that I may so share His sufferings"? This was the key to the transformation that I longed to see my clients experience and that I longed to know for myself.

What I deeply desired was fellowship with Jesus. I longed for intimacy with Him. I had said for many years that my determined purpose was to know Him. Why, then, had I not recognized that if I were to gain this longing of my heart, I must first taste His suffering? I *must* suffer. My Lord experienced pain in so many different ways—not just on the cross, but in the everyday ways that I suffer. To fully feel the pain we are given is to be drawn into the intimacy of what He knew and felt as He suffered. Here was my door to His heart.

I do not invite casual friends into my innermost life. Yet here I am being invited into the very heart of the living God, the God of Hosea 11 who lets Himself long and grieve and weep for His wandering creation. How could I resist, how could I not run with all that is in me into His arms? Like Paul, I cry, "I press on to take hold of that for which Christ Jesus took hold of me" (Philippians 3:12 AMP). But I hesitate. I do not run, because this path leads right into the fire—straight through the flood—right into the arms of shared suffering. That is where He is!

"'You will seek me and find me when you seek me with all your heart. I will be found by you,' declares the LORD..." (Jeremiah 29:13-14).

> Oh Lord, my heart shrinks back from suffering, demanding another road. So often I miss You because I do not want to walk into the Valley of the Shadow of Death. I want to walk with You in the joy-filled places, the spiritually high places. But You call me to the low places, for that is where You walked.

"For consider Him that endured such contradiction of sinners against Himself, lest ye be wearied and faint in your minds" (Hebrews 12:3 KJV).

An Aversion to Pain

Thomas a' Kempis, in *The Imitation of Christ*, states: "Jesus has many who love His kingdom in Heaven but few who bear His Cross.... They who love Jesus for His own sake, and not for the sake of comfort for themselves, bless Him in every trial and anguish of heart, no less than in the greatest joy."

In the first century, believing in Christ and becoming one of His own was often a death sentence. It was an invitation to persecution, hardship, tribulation, sorrow, pain—yes, even death. And yet in the midst of this great challenge, His followers were radiant and filled with courage and glory. They gladly walked to the lions in the arena or to the cross or the stake. Why is this different for us? We now grow angry with God if things do not go according to our plan. We have attempted to create heaven right here under our feet. When reality proves otherwise, we rage, demand an explanation, doubt the goodness of our Creator, and turn back.

Do We Even Need Heaven?

I once stayed in the newly acquired home of a good friend, an interior designer. She and her husband had just recently gutted the home, totally renovated it, and moved in. It was now all she wanted it to be. It was absolutely beautiful. She was sharing with me that she had just begun a study on Heaven. She said, "I haven't thought about Heaven for a very long time. I am realizing that this is because I have created heaven right here, and I don't want to leave it."

There it is! We do not know Jesus as we ought in this twenty-first century world, because we are committed to building heaven on earth. Oh, we may be firmly entrenched in the work of the ministry. But when asked to engage at the heart level, or when life crashes around our ears, something essential is missing for many of us. When *heaven now* proves false, people seek out pastor or counselor to help them find *heaven again*. We abandon painful marriages, try to "fix" our children, demand satisfying relationships, or insist on whatever change in circumstances we think might remedy our dissatisfaction.

What if Jesus had done that? His moment in Gethsemane, alone, would have been quickly altered. His conversation with the Father might have gone something like this: "Look, Father, I know we talked about this, but I didn't actually think You would take things this far! You *are* God, for heaven's sake! Change this situation now. I don't want to go through this kind of pain and agony for these pathetic humans. They've made their own choices, anyway. Do something! Get me out of this!" If this was Jesus' perspective as He prayed in these final hours, He might have said to His disciples, "What is this about? I asked you to watch with Me just one hour. You don't even care about Me! Why should I go through this agony for you when you aren't willing to pray with Me for one hour? You have no idea how you have hurt Me. I cannot continue in a relationship that is so one-sided and unfair. This is over—I'm out of here."

What about when Phillip asks to see the Father? Jesus might have said, "Phillip, have I been with you all this time and you still do not know Me? You do not really care about Me. If you cared about Me, you would want to understand Me. You would want to work on knowing Me. Obviously I don't really matter all that much to you. That's it. I am not going to be vulnerable to someone who is so insensitive." Do these words sound familiar? How unwilling you and I are to feel what He felt, to walk where He walked, and to find Him in the fellowship of a shared suffering.

I once asked a friend to be honest with one of his family members about the sin in his life. He agreed to do it. To prepare him for the reaction he might encounter, I asked, "What will you do if what you have been avoiding all along actually happens? What will you do if this person is shocked by your confession and rejects you?" His answer was quick and certain: "I will do my best to get out of the pain and move on."

Is that not the answer we most often give? We may not articulate it so clearly, but that is our strategy for dealing with the pain we encounter on a daily basis in relationships. This is not the right answer! We must enter the fellowship of His suffering if we are to know His heart. His greatest suffering was in the context of relationships. In the wilderness, temptation came from one Jesus had created and loved—one who had betrayed Him long before. The tempter had taken one-third of all of Christ's beloved angels with him.

In *Reliving the Passion,* Walter Wangerin, Jr. describes sorrow as that crucible at which the Father reshapes our superficial, fleeting happiness into deep and sustaining joy. Have we lived too long with shallow happiness, mistaking it for joy? As we explore our God Stories, could it be that God is inviting us to drink deeply of real joy? We can have this instead of a transient happiness that flees at the first taste of the sorrow of life lived outside the garden.

The Way of Brokenness

In 2 Corinthians 4:5-6, Paul tells the believers at Corinth that what he and his fellow servants preach "is not ourselves, but Jesus Christ as Lord, and ourselves as your servants for Jesus' sake." He tells them that God has displayed the light of the knowledge of Himself in the face of Jesus Christ and that their transformation into the Image of Christ will come by looking into His face. Paul goes on to explain a spiritual reality with an everyday metaphor, comparing them to jars of clay: While they hold the treasure of the image and the light of the presence of Jesus in their mortal bodies, they are not to take credit for it. This is so the glory might go to God and not to them.

What does this have to do with pain? Everything! Glory is best reflected in us when we are ordinary, not extraordinary; when we have touched our brokenness, not when we boast of our wholeness. We are clay pots so that we might "show that this all-surpassing power is from God and not from us" (2 Corinthians 4:7). If, as 2 Corinthians 1:3-4 testifies, I comfort others with the comfort God has used to comfort me, then I must have previously needed, and received, His comfort. How can I reflect Jesus to a lost and dying world, or even to my brother or sister who is struggling, if I have no knowledge of His presence in painful circumstances? The writer of Hebrews states that Jesus is a High Priest who can be touched with the feelings of our weaknesses, infirmities, and temptations. He was tempted in every respect as we are, yet He remained without sin. And so we are invited to fearlessly, confidently, and boldly draw near to the throne of God's unmerited favor to us sinners, that we may receive mercy for our failures and find grace to help with every need.

> Listen to what our Lord gave Jeremiah to say to us:
> Stand at the crossroads and look; ask for the ancient paths, ask where the good way is, and walk in it, and you will find rest for your souls. But you said, "We will not walk in it." (Jeremiah 6:16)

At that time, the children of Israel were called to a good path that promised them soul rest. This path, however, would not allow them to be in control. They rebelled, refusing to walk in the way of God's invitation. Like the Israelites, we are called to a path on which we will be revealed as broken vessels in the Potter's hand. It cannot be otherwise. We are walking demonstrations of the suffering, and therefore the grace, of God Most High. We can only declare what we have seen and heard to those around us.

Six hundred years later, God invited people no longer to follow a pathway, but a person:

> Come to Me, all you who labor and are heavy-laden and overburdened, and I will cause you to rest. [I will ease and relieve and refresh your souls.] Take My yoke upon you and learn of Me, for I am gentle (meek) and humble (lowly) in heart, and you will find rest (relief and ease and refreshment and recreation and blessed quiet) for your souls. For My yoke is wholesome (useful, good—not harsh, hard, sharp, or pressing, but comfortable, gracious, and pleasant), and My burden is light and easy to be borne. (Matthew 11:28-30 AMP)

With hearts prone to wander toward safety, we look to Jesus, who chose to walk a path of suffering for our benefit. Following in His footsteps, we find that our endurance in affliction benefits those for whom we pour out our lives. Do you hear the refrain? "Run!" "Come boldly!" "Come unto Me!" "So send I you." Are you grasping the picture? Pain is a part of life outside the garden. But, oh, the joy of running into the arms of Him Who captivates our souls with His beauty in the midst of that pain until we cry with bittersweet joy, "Lord, if this is what it takes to know You, if this is how I can experience You, if this is the place where Your presence and sweetness and overwhelming, eternal love ravish me, then may I never leave. Ignore my cries for relief!"

Paul talks about the oppressive distress that befell him and Timothy in Asia. He says that they despaired even of life itself; they felt that they had received the very sentence of death. However, Paul reflects that the purpose of this trouble was to keep them from depending on themselves instead of on God. Paul speaks honestly about hardship. But the conclusions he draws in the midst of pain reflect not bitterness, but relational hunger. He wants to find God far more than he wants tranquility or ease.

As I write this, the song *Follow Me,* by Ira F. Stamphill, has been running through my head. The lyrics describe yet another facet of the fellowship that comes from suffering:

> I've traveled down a lonely road and no one seemed to care,
> The burden on my weary back had bowed me to despair.

I've oft complained to Jesus how folks were treating me,
And then I heard Him say so tenderly:
"My feet were also weary upon the Calvary road,
The cross became so heavy I fell beneath the load.
Be faithful weary pilgrim the morning I can see,
Just lift your cross and follow close to Me."

"I work so hard for Jesus" I often boast and say,
"I've sacrificed a lot of things to walk the narrow way,
I gave up fame and fortune; I'm worth a lot to Thee."
And then I hear Him gently say to me,
"I left the throne of glory and counted it but loss,
My hands were nailed in anger upon a cruel cross,
But now we'll make the journey with your hand safe in Mine,
So lift your cross and follow close to Me."

Oh Jesus, if I die upon a foreign field someday,
T'would be no more than love demands, no less could I repay.
"No greater love hath mortal man than for a friend to die."
These are the words He gently spoke to me,
"If just a cup of water I place within your hand,
Then just a cup of water is all that I demand.
But if by death to living they can My glory see,
Then take your cross and follow close to Me."

How can we resist such an offer? How could I miss placing my hand in the hand of my Master? What a tragic loss! For this He died; for this we have been justified—to know Him not only in the power of His resurrection, but also in the fellowship of His suffering. May we not shrink back! We do believe; help our unbelief, Lord Jesus (Mark 9:24).

Pain is God's handwritten, blood-engraved invitation to intimacy. This is true regardless of the specific nature or source of our pain. Your pain, wherever you are in this moment, is exactly where your loving Lord, Husband, and Shepherd wants to meet you. May you have eyes to see the One who is drawing, wooing, and loving you, Who longs to feed, nurture, enjoy, and be enjoyed by you. It is when you yield in utter obedience to His sovereignty in your life that your eyes meet His eyes looking intently into yours. Then you begin to love as you are loved. Then you taste the water of life satisfying your thirsty soul. As the Lover in Song of Solomon, He is inviting you to respond to His invitation to come away with Him, to anchor yourself in the reality that you are His beloved.

COMPASS CHECK

- *List some painful experiences that you have responded to with avoidance. What results did these lead to?*
- *List some painful experiences that you embraced in obedience to God. How did these turn out?*
- *In what ways are you seeking to turn your life on earth into your own version of heaven?*
- *How do these attempts distract you from your true calling in Christ?*

Chapter 4
Encounters

The Father, Son and Holy Spirit,
after much deliberation and forethought, made a decision to create man.
They would create them in their Image and Likeness
and they would create them Male and Female.
Genesis 1:27, Author's paraphrase

THE MIRROR

Imagine with me that on the 6th day of creation, God stood in front of a gigantic mirror, a metaphor which perfectly reflected His Image. There in all its glory was reflected the nature, character and person of the Triune God. The time had come to call forth humankind, the pinnacle of creation. With a word, God shattered the mirror into pieces as numerous as the sands on every seashore and all the stars in the heavens. No two pieces were the same. "These," He said, "will individually and collectively reflect our glory into the world we have created. Each one will bear something different of Our Image to reflect into time, space and history. Each story will hone and refine the aspect of Our character borne by the individual." When I think of this I can't help wondering, could it be that the white stone referred to in Revelation 2:17 and the name written on it will bring into focus the aspect of the image borne by the one who receives it?

And here we are, each created to reflect the image of God in a way that no one else has, can, or ever will. In this lies the truth of our uniqueness: together we are created to reflect the image of God into the world. Each individual has been entrusted to bear an aspect of the image of God that has never been seen before and will never be seen again until glory. The Godhead delights in being known in this way and in watching His created beings become all they were created to be. However, this is not the full story. The enemy of our souls—the one who accuses us—has seen this uniqueness and hates us for it.

The Creator, the Enemy, and the Image Bearer

Tradition holds that Satan rebelled against God before man was created. But imagine with me again: could it have gone another way? What if Satan revolted after he saw Adam, rather than before? What if it was when he saw Adam that he finally realized he really could never be like God? He had seen the face of God; he had lived and served and worshiped in God's presence. He was called the Morning

Star. Could his choice to rebel have been precipitated by the horrifying realization that Adam, not he, was created to reflect the image of God? Could this have been the moment he realized that he was simply a servant: not only of God, but also of Adam, this "like-God one"? This realization would have enraged Satan. Not only was he not like God, but he was created to serve God's image bearers, something he was loath to do. He hated the fact that they had what he so wanted for himself. If he could not be like God, he would see to it that they couldn't either. His hatred was both for the One whom he could never be and for those who reflected His perfect image.

Isaiah captures the fallen beauty of God's creation, Satan: the height of his fall, the vow showing the direction of his heart, and the establishment of a kingdom in opposition to God's intended rule:

> How have you fallen from heaven, O light-bringer and daystar, son of the morning! How you have been cut down to the ground, you who weakened and laid low the nations [O blasphemous, satanic king of Babylon!]
>
> And you said in your heart, I will ascend to heaven; I will exalt my throne above the stars of God; I will sit upon the mount of assembly in the uttermost north. I will ascend above the heights of the clouds; I will make myself like the Most High. Yet you shall be brought down to Sheol (Hades), to the innermost recesses of the pit (the region of the dead). (Isaiah 14:12-15 AMP)

It is clear that Satan's commitment is to exalt himself, to undercut God, and to leave as much human collateral as he can. He is angry and is hungry for power, fame, and a God-likeness that he can imitate but will never truly possess. He has been allowed freedom, but this freedom is not eternal. He will be judged along with us at the end of this age. Still, he is a foe to be reckoned with.

When Satan meets Eve in the garden, he calls into question what is true about her by adding an aspect which she knows is forbidden: "You could be like God, knowing good and evil" (Genesis 3:5). While Adam and Eve were already like God in many ways and had been created to reflect the very image of God, they did not yet know the difference between good and evil. With Satan's words, the very essence of Eve's being as an image bearer was brought into question, and she was tempted with the desire to be someone on her own apart from God. She would be like God in a different way than He had conferred upon her; she could be like God, knowing what God knows. She would not ever have to ask Him anything.

Rebellion

Satan's rebellious activities did not end in the garden. He continues to deceive us in the same way he deceived Eve—by casting doubt on the character and integrity of God. "Can it really be that God has said…?" he subtly asks. Upon hearing Eve's version of God's instruction, he countered, "You will not surely die." In this conversation, Eve was seduced into believing a lie. Adam, in turn, chose to disobey God. By his disobedience, he chose who he would honor as god, putting himself and Eve under Satan's rule. He handed the dominion he had under God's headship to Satan, and Satan became the god of this world.

Adam and Eve knew what it was like to gaze upon God and to feel His gaze directly. Every evening they would walk together through the garden that they stewarded in partnership, watching the animals that Adam had named and admiring the plants that grew in fruitful abundance. With the choice to rebel against God's simple mandate about the tree of knowledge, they were left to live out their lives separated from the shameless intimacy their souls had been created for. Eve would begin to demand that Adam offer her what God had provided in the Garden. Adam would feel appropriately inadequate and fearful, because no matter how hard he tried, he could not be God for Eve. In addition, no matter how hard he tried, the wind, the waves, and the weeds would never obey his voice again.

Our Part in this Story

In Evangelical Christianity we have been told, for the most part, that Satan isn't really concerned with us; he hates the God who loves us, and toying with us is simply a way to spite God. I believe this is only partly true; the enemy of our souls does hate God, but he also, in fact, hates us. He is committed to seeing that if he cannot be like God, neither can we. Furthermore, he is dedicated to establishing a kingdom which undercuts God's Kingdom and invites us to join his rebellion. As our reward for participation in this revolt, he offers to help us manage our lives to the end that we become our own gods. While Satan is unable to create, he does work craftily to twist the truth about who he is, who we are, and who God is. Satan is a pretender, masquerading as an angel of light (2 Corinthians 11:14), seeking to divert our attention from the true Light of the World (John 8:12). Meanwhile God, in whom there is no darkness at all (1 John 1:5), calls us to bring His true light to the world (Matthew 5:14).

Who Will Be God?

And here we find ourselves, daughters of Eve and sons of Adam, living outside the garden, in need of a god: created human beings cannot be their own gods. And we find Satan, and all the dark hordes of fallen angels with him, working to convince us that God cannot be trusted. We need someone to protect us from our fears and provide for us our longings; however, the God who created us for Himself seems too unpredictable and unsafe to be trusted. And so, we take up our shields and swords to protect and fight for ourselves. Here the enemy steps in to remind us that we are unable to manage without a god. He is willing to let us sit as a figurehead as long as he is the one in control. In effect, he says, "You are going to need help getting what you want and protecting yourself from what you fear. I will help you." Our assent is rarely a conscious decision, but that does not make the weight of it any lighter or its effects any less potent.

How does the enemy do this? In my own story there were many childhood events which communicated that I was not wanted. I either heard people say or saw reflected in their actions that I was not as good as others. I was clearly missing something that others had, although I had no idea what that something was. It seemed that someone else was always asked to the party instead of me; someone else was thinner, prettier, funnier, or in some other way more desirable. And so I decided that I would have to protect myself from the pain of that awareness.

When I took up my shield, the enemy stepped in and said, "You will need a god to protect you. But you're in luck—I can help you. Tell you what… Every time someone is about to find out that you have nothing to offer that they want, I will step in and remind you not to offer anything, to be careful, to back away. Listen closely for my voice. Whenever you are at risk of being hurt, I will quietly remind you: 'Be careful! Have you forgotten who you are? They will find out if you step forward.'" And so I would participate on the sidelines hoping that someone would see and invite me in, while at the same time being convinced that they never would. The enemy had quietly and effectively secured a foothold in my life. I had made an agreement to allow him to use fear and shame to keep me hidden. It worked well, and I avoided the worst of what I feared, but at what cost? The piece of the mirror that I am, the unique reflection of the Trinity that I bring to the world, was obscured. I was effectively veiling the image, character, nature, and person of God that I bring to time, space and history. The very thing that God had given me to reflect to the world was now hidden in fear and shame. Like Moses, I had veiled my face to hide the radiant glory of God that was mine to reflect. The enemy had narrowed his focus and gone right to my strength. The thing I must never offer is my passion. But I am running ahead of myself. How, you ask, did he do that? To answer this, I must share with you another part of my God Story.

A Wound and A Choice

In the third grade, I was chosen to be the lead in a Christmas play that was restricted to fourth through sixth graders. You can imagine how special I felt! I memorized things easily, and this part had a lot of lines. I relished practicing all of them, imagining myself under the spotlight. The story was set in the state of Montana, where I grew up. My character was a girl who moved to Florida and was determined to find a way for Santa Claus to deliver her gifts, despite the lack of chimneys.

On the night of the play, my debut was finally at hand. All of my practicing and memorizing would pay off. My father, my leading man, was in the audience. He was known in the community as a very talented actor, as well as a musician and vocalist, and I adored him. I couldn't wait for him to see me be like him and show the world that I was his daughter. I loved who he was and I admired his passion for the things he had accomplished as an actor. I was also passionate and dramatic and loved every minute in the spotlight. What I did not understand then was that he couldn't value my passion, because he didn't know how to value his own.

For a full hour I was center-stage in a star-studded, navy blue swimsuit. I was surrounded by toys and animals, all there because of me. Could anything be more perfect for an eight-year-old? I was in my glory, with every ounce of the passion I possessed—and a good deal of over-acting, I suspect—poured into that role.

When the play was over I headed directly for my dad in the school lobby. He was with my mother and my beloved grandmother. I ran up to him with all the excitement and hope my little heart could contain, bursting to ask him if he was pleased. "Daddy, Daddy, did you like me, was I good?" My father looked at me but did not answer my question. His face was hard. Silently, he turned to my mother, said, "Get her dressed and get her out of here," and walked out of the school. I felt dizzy. Claws of shame, shock, and confusion sank into my eight-year-old heart. I had poured my passion out before my father, and he had smothered it with contempt. At that moment, I knew only one thing: I would never be humiliated in that way again.

Throughout my school years, I had drama teachers, thespian sponsors and others who encouraged me to get into drama. As a junior in high school, my English teacher offered me extra credit if I would memorize two dramatic readings and compete in a dramatic reading competition. I memorized the readings. I performed them in front of my mirror over and over and over, getting them just right. I knew I could shine. However, I never received the extra credit, because I refused to perform them in front of a single human being. How could I bear the thought that others, seeing what my father had seen, might confirm my greatest fear?

On that winter night, my father had unwittingly communicated that my passion was despicable. From then on, I refused to believe anything else. I was too afraid. The person I was created to be was fatally flawed; I must veil it to survive. The enemy of my soul—the enemy of Him who would one day become my Savior—had convinced me to cover my unique piece of the mirror in fear of the pain of what others would say. And so he won: no one would see the special facet of God's image that I had been given to offer the world.

For many years, I was ruled by the terror of offering myself. I felt stuck, unable to move, a victim of my circumstances. But soon after I turned 40, the light slowly began to dawn. I began to understand my part in the transaction I had made. I saw my commitment to control the pain in my world by living defensively and managing my circumstances. My guard was always up. I knew how to offer what I thought people wanted, but not who I really was. While I had been young at the time of my wounding and was not responsible for the ways my father sinned against me, I had yet chosen to follow Eve into a life of stubborn self-protection. Even as a youngster, I had been given a choice as to who I would allow to protect me, and I had enlisted help from someone other than God. I had unwittingly given the enemy a foothold in my life.

These realizations began to unfold for me during my time at Grace Theological Seminary as I sat under the teaching of Dr. Charles Smith. He taught us that the key to the stronghold in this fight and to the healing that followed came in learning to question where the enemy first achieved his stronghold; the root must be attacked, then the branches would follow. In my own life and in the lives of those around me, I saw clear evidence that this was the only way to become free—free to offer the world who we were created to be. However, it was not until I read *Waking the Dead* by John Eldredge that the pieces came together for me. Of course we are in enemy territory: the Scriptures make clear that we are in a battle. To fight well, we need to understand where we are, who our enemy is, and what weapons are ours to wield.

Obedience: Better Than Sacrifice

The age-old story of King Saul illustrates the implications of my choice to rebel against God. Saul was anointed by God to be the first king over the children of Israel. God placed on Saul His favor, blessing, protection, and authority. However, Saul's willingness to obey was not unconditional. Saul honored and obeyed God when it made practical sense to him, but otherwise, Saul played by his own rules. This did not escape God's notice, and God tested Saul in order to reveal the contents of his heart. When God tests us, it is not so He can discover the nature of our affections. He needs no one to tell Him what is in the heart of each man. He knows every heart and every thought, before the one who thinks it realizes its weight. God does not test us for His own benefit, but so that we can see our motives for ourselves.

In I Samuel we read of the test: God commands Saul to wipe out the Amalekites, sworn enemies of God and His chosen people. Giving Saul God's message, the prophet Samuel states that after the conquest he is to kill every living thing, human and animal. He is to bring nothing back alive. He is even to kill King Agag. But Saul and his men do not obey God. "[They] spared Agag and the best of the sheep and cattle, the fat calves and lambs—everything that was good. These they were unwilling to destroy completely, but everything that was despised and weak they totally destroyed" (I Samuel 15:9).

When God alerts Samuel to Saul's disobedience, he spends the night crying out to God. The next morning he set off to find Saul, only to discover that Saul has gone down to Carmel to build a monument in his own honor. Upon Samuel's arrival, Saul greet him with a blessing and the affirmation that he has carried out the Lord's instructions. When Samuel asks him to explain the sound of bleating sheep, Saul shifts blame to the soldiers: it was their idea—not his—to bring the king and animals back. If you listen closely, you can hear the echoes of Adam's defense in the Garden of Eden. When faced with our own culpability, we most often blame others for our disobedience.

Samuel's words to Saul in 1 Samuel 15:22-23 are sobering even today. I will paraphrase for emphasis:

> Has the Lord as great a delight in burnt offerings and sacrifices as in obeying His voice? To obey is better than sacrifice and to listen to Him is better than the fat of any ram. Your rebellion is as the sin of witchcraft and your stubbornness is as idolatry. Because you have rejected the word of the Lord, He has rejected you from being king. He has removed you from the favored status, under the protection and blessing of His authority. Because you have rejected the Lord as your master, He has rejected you as king.

Jesus' words echo Samuel's injunction, speaking to the timelessness of this story: 'You cannot serve two masters: You will hate the one and love the other' (Matthew 6:24, author's paraphrase). Although Jesus was speaking of money as the second master, the root of both is an autonomous, willful choice to be the one in control. That is where Saul placed himself: rebelling against the authority of the

Lord and therefore clinging to the other god whose authority he had bowed to by his disobedience. And this is what I had done: given the enemy authority in my life to protect me from what I feared the most.

Life Outside the Garden

But what should I do? I knew that something was wrong. People were asking me to teach them what I knew about being a soul-care shepherd, but I refused. To teach would call my passion into the light, and I would be exposed. I could not risk that. From 1989 to 1992, three retired teachers begged me to teach them to help the wounded girls they were meeting with. And for three years, I said, "No!"

Then, one day as I was spending time with God, He opened my eyes to the rebellion that was fueling my fear-filled decision to hide. He told me, "Patti, I want you to come out of hiding. These women need your help." I was faced with a choice. But what would happen if I came out of hiding? How would people respond when they saw what my father saw? Again, I heard God speak: "Dear One, I am calling you to use what I have given you as I intended you to use it. If they see you as you do, you will need to leave that to Me." I had a choice. I could either bow my knee to the God of the Universe or continue to choose to stubbornly protect myself. And so I placed a phone call and committed myself to teaching the class I had been avoiding. This was a practical act of repentance, telling God that I would live from who He had made me to be. I would leave behind the imposter-self that the enemy had so long helped me to maintain.

I could not have known then how my decision to once again bow my knee to my Creator and trust His heart toward me would shape my life. Ever since agreeing to teach that class, I have been training people to care for the souls of others. My passion is both what I continue to grow into and live out of. And this began with taking back the territory I had unknowingly given to the enemy of my soul.

To speak of reclaiming ground from the enemy acknowledges that we are in the midst of a battle. My husband, John, and I continue to recognize ways that we have given our allegiance to the corrupted one in hopes of being spared from chaos outside of the Garden of Eden. And so we have learned to battle together, on behalf of each other. We have practiced putting on and using the armor of Ephesians 6. We may live in enemy territory, but it is our choice whether or not we will fight.

Reclaiming Lost Ground

James' book of wisdom concludes with an exhortation toward purity in the face of suffering. He acknowledges to his readers that there is a battle taking place and that this battle must be fought actively, with great measures of humility. The deals we make with the enemy of our souls to gain protection are born of pride.

> You adulterous people, don't you know that friendship with the world means enmity against God? Therefore, anyone who chooses to be a friend of the world becomes an enemy of God. Or do you think Scripture says without reason that he jealously longs for the Spirit he has caused to dwell in us? But he gives us more grace. That is why Scripture says: "God opposes the proud but shows favor to the humble." *Submit yourselves, then, to God. Resist the devil, and he will flee from you.* Come near to God and he will come near to you. Wash your hands, you sinners, and purify your hearts, you double-minded. Grieve, mourn and wail. Change your laughter to mourning and your joy to gloom. Humble yourselves before the Lord, and he will lift you up. (James 4:4-10, italics mine)

In the past, I confidently told people that if they resisted the devil, he would flee from them. Their response to me was puzzling: "I have done that, and it hasn't worked." Upon reflection, I realized that I had also experienced the same mixed outcome. Sometimes I found freedom, and other times I didn't. Why? A pastor friend drew my attention to the fact that I was skipping the first part of James 4:7. We first needed to submit ourselves to God. How could something like that have escaped my notice? What I have seen in the lives of men and women since that realization has been nothing short of miraculous. The enemy has fled and has not returned to any area once it is submitted to God. There may still be other pieces of ground to reclaim from the enemy, yes. But what the Scriptures say is true. If we acknowledge the brokenness of our own attempts to make life work without God, submitting to Him and resisting the enemy, we will draw near to God; He eagerly waits to draw near to us. How abundant is His care toward us! There will always be enough grace for us to experience this abundance, if only we are willing.

Let me explain how this played out in my own story. When I resisted the devil in the authority of the Name of Jesus Christ and told him to flee, I encountered a pushback that went something like this: "Patti, you cannot come to me and tell me to flee in the authority of the Name of Jesus Christ. What are you thinking? This area is not under the authority of Jesus. You put this area under my authority, remember? You saw that you could not trust Jesus to protect you from the wounds of others when you lived out of your heart of passion, so we entered a covenant of protection: my protection for your submission. You veil your face, and I will remind you—protect you—with fear and shame. You will be safe, and I get to be god. What better deal could there be?" Here is my response, as I cried out to God in journaling prayer:

> O Lord, what have I done? What do I need to do? **Child, you must obey what you see in James: you must submit to Me.** Submit *what* to You, Lord? **You must bow your knee to the reality that what happened when your father saw your passion could happen again. You must bow your knee to the fact that it may be to MY greatest glory that this happen again and again. If I can best reveal Myself through you this way, will you bow your knee to Me? Will you let Me be your protector? Will you let Me decide what comes to you and what does not?**
> Yes, Abba, I will do that. I bow my knee to Your supreme authority in my life – You are the Potter; I am the clay. Make what You will. **Patti, you are now back under the Authority of the Name of the Lord Jesus Christ in this area. You may use His name and tell the enemy he no longer has the power to protect you. Tell the enemy that you will bow to any pain I allow in your life. Resist him, renounce the commitment to him and tell him to flee. Now he has no choice. You are under My protection and the hedge of My Authority will surround you. You are free.** Thank You, Father. **Now do what the rest of the verse says: Draw near to Me – you have pushed Me away as Saul did, but no longer. You have cleared the way for Me to draw near to you. Remember child; if you seek Me with all your heart, I will be found by you.**

A word on fighting this type of spiritual battle: no one else can command a demon to leave if you yourself have retained his services—wittingly or unwittingly. You must speak to him yourself. Many will remind me that even Michael the archangel did not rebuke Satan, but asked God to rebuke him. But we are different from the angels and have been given authority to wage war in the heavenly realms. Michael is an angel, a servant of image bearers and the Most High God. Because of this, he does not have the same authority as image bearers. Paul, Peter, and Jesus, however, spoke directly to the demons. We may as well.

Peter's first letter to the churches that were located in what is now Turkey concludes with an exhortation to be aware of the real presence of an enemy. This is an opportunity to trust, to not fear, and to actively fight. Again, there is a call to humility in the face of this battle:

> All of you, clothe yourselves with humility toward one another, because, "God opposes the proud but shows favor to the humble." Humble yourselves, therefore, under God's mighty hand, that he may lift you up in due time. Cast all your anxiety on him because he cares for you. Be alert and of sober mind. Your enemy the devil prowls around like a roaring lion looking for someone to devour. Resist him, standing firm in the faith, because you know that the family of believers throughout the world is undergoing the same kind of sufferings. And the God of all grace, who called you to his eternal glory in Christ, after you have suffered a little while, will himself restore you and make you strong, firm and steadfast. To him be the power for ever and ever. Amen. (1 Peter 5:5-10)

Remember where you are and Whose you are. Adam gave up his rule of this earth to Satan, the Prince of the power of the air, the ruler of darkness in high places. As a result, we are living in the domain of the god of this world. We are in the enemy's territory, like the Jews in Nazi Germany, and it would behoove us to be aware of this reality. Recognize that you have an enemy who hates you and hates the One who made you. Recognize also that you are a target of the one who hates you because you uniquely reflect a glory that he hates. Ask the Spirit of God to search your heart and shine light on those places where you have rejected God and have asked another to protect you. Where are the places you live in fear, anger, rebellion, or pride? How have you refused to surrender to Jesus as your Lord? Where in your life is He not enthroned? Your enemy has set himself against God's incarnation in you. He will work all of his wiles to convince you that he can protect you better than your Maker. Jesus called us to be wise as serpents and harmless as doves. We have been equipped with the whole armor of God so that we can resist the enemy's deception. Do not be like the man who beholds in a mirror his own image and then walks away and immediately forgets (James 1:24). Ask the Spirit of God to draw you to Himself in ways you do not even know you need and yet your spirit longs for.

Nearly two thousand years ago, St. Irenaeus wrote, "The Glory of God is man fully alive." Only in the life that our Creator offers can we experience the freedom and safety we long for. The protection offered by the enemy can only imitate what we were created to experience. While this does not mean we will be free from pain, it does mean that the pain we touch in our lives is well within the Redeemer's reach. He will use it to draw us deeply into intimacy with Himself. He is the God who restores.

Lord God, it thrills my heart to realize the uniqueness You have placed in me, and the possibilities of what this means for my life. And yet there are parts of me that shrink back, where I think that I have allowed the enemy room to roam. When I consider this, God, I feel defeated already. And yet, if what You say is true, by inviting the Spirit to show me the ways I have refused to bow my knee to You, I can learn to walk in the freedom You created me for. I acknowledge the deaths that I must die for this to happen: my longings for comfort and safety, my longings to determine my influence, my many strategies to make life work without You.

Oh Lord, save me from myself. Your jealousy for my whole heart is a righteous jealousy, and I confess to You my unfaithfulness, my pride, and my pursuit of other lovers. I want to learn to trust You more than I do now, and to learn to live with an unveiled face before You and the world You have placed me in. Come as the Restorer, the Redeemer, and bring Your steadfastness to replace what I have chosen. How I long to walk in the garden with You, in the cool of the day, talking with You as one does with a friend. I choose to believe that You are good, even when You are not safe. Help me to live into the expansiveness my heart was created for and to welcome You back to where You have always belonged.

COMPASS CHECK

Looking back on your life, what are some critical moments in which you have made decisions to turn away from God, receiving help (either knowingly or unknowingly) from the enemy to stay safe?

Once you begin writing your God Story, make sure you include these important incidents in your timeline. Discuss them with God and submit the affected areas of your life to your heavenly Father. In the name of Jesus Christ, tell the enemy that you no longer want his "help" and that these parts of your life are no longer under his domain but belong to Jesus.

Chapter 5
Forks in the Road

Be alert and of sober mind.
Your enemy the devil prowls around like a roaring lion
looking for someone to devour.
1 Peter 5:8

TWO VOICES

God's creativity includes the way He uses whatever is available to Him in our lives to bring our hearts alive to Himself. As you write your God Story, you will find unexpected places where your heart recognizes the presence of God. You are not alone, but rather are joining many others who are surprised by God's presence. At the end of Luke, the disciples who were walking on the road to Emmaus found this to be true as Jesus joined them on their journey (Luke 24:13-32). They were talking about the Passover-unlike-any-Passover that had just occurred in Jerusalem and were captivated as their new companion (who they only later realized was Jesus) knit the stories together from the Scriptures and made clear all that the men had not been able to make sense of. Later, after they realized that their companion had been Jesus, they asked each other, "Were not our hearts burning within us as we walked with Him on the road?" As the two men looked back upon their encounter with Jesus on the Emmaus Road, they realized what had really happened: God had been there. This is a key component in writing your own God Story. Where did you feel your heart burn? Are there things that bring you back to those places?

A dear friend was journaling through a passage of Scripture in dialogue form, conversing with God about what was written there. She was part of a group which had gathered to listen for the voice of God spoken through His Word. During the writing time, wind chimes were stirred outside. A deep peace settled over her soul, a peace she associated with the confirmation of God's presence in past experiences. When we gathered together after our time alone with God, she shared, "I did not hear Him speak to me, but even if I had I would have thought it was my own voice in my head." And yet she had heard Him. As a group, we were like the men talking together, who realized they had met Jesus on the road. It was thrilling to realize with her: Jesus knew the way He had found to make His presence and His voice known. His voice was in the chimes; her heart recognized the sound of His voice and knew peace.

Another dear sister had found a taste of life and beauty in dance and music as a child. Her heart was forever captured by the music of the dance. Through time and difficult circumstances, the soil of this friend's life had become arid; she had come to wonder whether God really existed. One day she walked into a room in which a man was playing the dance music she loved most. She was moved to tears and had to leave the room. She had unexpectedly heard the voice of the Lover of her soul, Who had kept her heart alive to His voice in the music. He never left Himself without a way to reach her heart.

As you write your story, ask yourself these questions: *what causes my heart to burn, to make it feel most alive? What did I love as a child*? Was it the wind in your face as you rode your bike? The sound of a baseball game as you sat next to your dad to watch it with him? The smell of pine trees and a campfire burning somewhere in the forest? In what experiences does God want you to see that He was present?

As you recall experiences of pleasure and longing, it is important to recognize that these are indications of the presence of God. Looking back, it may seem that a gaping hole exists where you wish a loving God had been. This is a very real feeling if there are places where you don't see Him, especially if bad things were happening to you. And yet Psalm 139 not only says that you were formed with purpose and intention, but that God was present with you from conception. Perhaps this is easier to believe for others than for yourself; in fact, you may find yourself listening to the voice that says that this was absolutely not true for you. And yet Numbers 23:19 says that "God is not human, that he should lie, not a human being, that he should change his mind. Does he speak and then not act? Does he promise and not fulfill?" We can believe that if He says that He was there, sitting with you wherever you were, then He *was* there. Remember how Jesus knew the heart and life of the woman in John 4 although they had never met before.

Not only was He there, but He was using whatever was available to Him to draw your attention to His presence and to the sound of His voice. He spoke to people on your behalf, asking them not to treat you unkindly. He asked people to protect you, fight for you, and love you. Too often these people declined because of their own sin. In so doing, they sinned against you. Nevertheless, He found ways to waken your heart to the burning awareness of His presence. Oh, you did not yet know that it was His presence. Perhaps you did not know that He even existed. Still, He wooed you, called your name, and spoke tenderly to you. It thrills His heart that you are traveling back into your story to find the places where He longs to be found.

In I Samuel 3, the Lord calls out to the child Samuel, but Samuel has not yet learned to recognize His voice. Because he has never heard God speak, Samuel thinks that Eli is calling him. He runs to Eli, but Eli answers that he has not called him. Samuel goes back to bed and again hears the voice. Samuel once again goes to Eli. Eli tells him that perhaps he is hearing the voice of God, and the next time he hears the voice, he should say, "Speak, Lord, for Your servant hears." And he does.

Young Samuel needed someone who knew God to help him identify the voice of God. That he did not recognize the voice as God's does not change that God had and was continuing to speak to him. You, like Samuel, have heard the voice of God but may not know how to recognize it as such. As you write your God Story, ask Him to identify the sound of His voice. He will. He does not speak in order to hide Himself, but so that we will learn to hear Him. Like Samuel, you may need someone who knows the voice of God to listen to your story and help you recognize God's voice. However, soon enough, you will become familiar with the sound of His voice and respond with a joy that can only be described as *"a burning in your heart."*

One of the significant lessons I have learned from *Learning to Love the Master* is that God is always speaking to my heart. I have come to expect God to converse with me and have learned to identify the burning in my heart that accompanies His voice. I continue to learn not to ignore it. Like young Samuel, I respond, "Speak, Lord, your servant listens."

Writing your God Story not only helps you to recognize God's presence and listen for His voice but also gives you an opportunity to identify the lies the enemy has spoken into your life. Revelation 12:10 tell us that this enemy is called the Accuser of the brethren. He lives to make accusations, and nothing is off limits: he accuses you to yourself, he accuses you to God, he accuses God to you, he accuses you to others and he accuses others to you. I am using the name Satan to include the fallen angels under his authority.

When I read Psalm 139, it is clear that if the Creator has been with you since He knit you together in your mother's womb, then He was also present in your delivery room with you. It seems to follow that the god of this world—your Accuser—was very likely there, too. I suspect that ever since the fall of Adam and Eve, Satan has been prowling in order to accuse people at the very first chance he can get. Keep in mind that he knows the face of God. Because of this, he recognizes immediately what it is that God has imprinted of Himself on you. That makes his job a lot easier, because it is the one thing he must convince you is not true about yourself—he takes one look at you and understands the specific accusation he must level in your direction. Satan is not so foolish as to leave you alone until you are an adult and then start lying to you. No, he is counting on the fact that as a child, you are a concrete thinker with very little knowledge or understanding of the world. He attacks you before you are able to recognize the lies. While not very original, he *is* crafty. His message will probably resonate with what he said to Eve: "You could be like God, and really, when you think about it, are you sure that you can trust God to protect you from this pain you feel living outside the garden? Trust me, and I will make sure that your life goes well."

And yet Satan *doesn't* make sure your life goes well. In fact, he can't. He is solely committed to twisting the image of God in you to a place where you no longer reflect your Creator, whom he hates. As the father of lies, Satan is not one who keeps his word. He has set out to tell you his version of who you are, masquerading as a false Jesus. He has reminded you over and over again that you have fallen short and told you that no one will ever love you or want you if you are not careful. He has convinced you that you are going to need his help to keep others from seeing you the way you see yourself; feeling about you the way you feel about yourself. But by this point, "who you are" is who he has recreated your image to be according to *his* purpose.

Consider this: haven't almost all the voices said the same thing to you in one way or another throughout your life? There is a good chance that Satan has not only been creating an image for you to embrace, but that he has been saying the same thing about you to all those around you. Remember, he *is* the "accuser of the brethren."

Recognizing the Voice of the Enemy

This voice is also accompanied by a visceral experience. Instead of the 'burning heart' experience of God's presence, there is the 'shamed, sick heart' feeling at the presence of the despiser of our souls. When painful, embarrassing, humiliating events come up in your story, what goes on viscerally—in your gut? Shame causes you to feel like someone has pulled your plug out of the electrical socket—you are powerless, frozen. You cannot move; you may even feel unable to think clearly. Your only desire is to have the floor open and swallow you up. If only you could be invisible!

For years, upon remembering some humiliating event, I would flush red and begin to perspire as if that event were happening in the current moment. Immediately, I would fly into a mental argument, defending and explaining myself, raging, and pouring contempt on the people in my memory. All this was an attempt to fight my way out of shame.

Shame has to do with the eyes of another seeing our nakedness. Adam and Eve were the first to experience this, and they hid in response, assembling fig leaves to cover themselves. We do the same thing. Our "fig leaves" may be more sophisticated than theirs, but they serve the same purpose.

As a child, the enemy used my father's voice to convince me that I should hide the mirror piece God had given me to reflect. Speaking of my heartfelt tears as false, he would say, "Your bladder is too close to your eyes." Communicating that I had nothing important to say, he told me, "You are a three act play," "You don't have the sense God gave geese" and, "Patti, you talk to hear yourself talk!" What did I know but to believe him? He was my father, the one God had placed in my life to tell me who I am. He was the one commissioned to be God's representative. He was the mirror given to reflect the truth about me. As my father, he was my God-figure.

Looking into the mirror of a parent's responses can be like seeing your reflection in a distorted carnival mirror. You may not gain any real sense of who you are. The true reflection of God's image in us that our parents are called to give has been warped by the pain they have suffered, their sin, and the lies the enemy has told *them*. We must remember that there is a war going on. The keys to death and hell have been taken away from the devil, and his time is coming to an end. He is screaming at you from every direction, telling you that only *he* can make sure your deep longings will be met.

As you write your God Story, be alert for the lies the enemy is speaking. This "second voice" is the most dangerous voice in the universe. It is the voice of the one who hates. He hates God, because he jealously wants supremacy. He hates you because you are like God. If Satan cannot be like God and was, in fact, created only to serve the image bearers carrying God's imprint, then he will see to it that you live without knowledge of that imprint. He will trick you while you are too young to know any better. He will weave his messages into your circumstances and relationships. He will whisper lies to you about who God has made you to be. He did the same thing with Eve: "You could be like God," he said, when she already *was* like God. He mis-interpreted God's words to Eve in order to change her perception of the truth.

Still, there is the voice of the One described in Psalm 139—the One who knows you and sits with you. The One who gently rests His hand on you. The One who is always closest to you. Close your eyes, rest your hand on your chest, and turn your eyes inward; that is where you will find Him. Long before you believed on Him for salvation, He was present and speaking. And now, if you have confessed your sin to Him with a heart of repentance and put your faith in Him, receiving the sacrifice Jesus Christ made for your salvation, God's Holy Spirit dwells in you. He is most intimately with you and can always be found. He will never leave you nor forsake you.

> After a group of us had gathered to listen for Your voice spoken through Your Word, I wrote: "Abba, it is very hard to wrap our hearts and minds around this notion of Two Voices. Thank You for the clarity You gave regarding the theme of Voice as the experience of a 'burning heart' when we encounter You in our story. You brought to mind things You had used to touch that 'burning place' in our hearts, just like the disciples on the Emmaus Road: music, chimes, the sound of a dog barking, the smell of rain, the ocean, the mountains, the Word, a doll held, a small animal, the sound of a voice, a room where we felt safe, and a myriad of other sights and sounds and places."

Praying the Armor of God

From Ephesians 6:10-20

Finally, be strong in the Lord and in his mighty power.
Put on the full armor of God,
so that you can take your stand against the devil's schemes.
Ephesians 6:10-11

Father of Holiness, place on our heads the helmet of salvation.
Guard our minds. May we experience the safety of knowing moment by moment Whose we are. Remind us that we belong to You. Speak to us of the three-fold belonging: we are handmade… blood-bought… wooed and won. If there are any further ways of belonging to You, draw us also into those kinds of belonging.

Gird our waists with the belt of truth.
May we experience the support and protection of being surrounded and tightly embraced by the Truth. May we hear truth, see truth, discern truth, love truth, speak truth, follow truth, and live out truth in every possible way. May the lies of the enemy, the lies from the world, and the lies from within have no authority over our lives. May we be captivated by the beauty of truth. May He who is Faithful and True live out His life in and through us. May we joyfully come under His authority.

Buckle on us the breastplate of righteousness.
May we find safety in **right standing** and **right doing**: right standing with You, Sovereign Lord, through the blood of Christ; and right doing by the power of Your Holy Spirit. By Your grace, and as a gift, please remove from us handholds the enemy has gained, even ones he has gained legally. Weaken and tear down strongholds the enemy has built within. Cause us to hunger and thirst for righteousness. By Your mercy, grant us repentance as needed.

Cover our feet with the preparation of the gospel of peace.
Prepare us to speak peace. Put on us the shoes of reconciliation so that we can walk in peace with You, with others, and within ourselves. Grant us grace to make amends where necessary. May we live the gospel of reconciliation in such a way that when we speak the gospel of reconciliation to lost souls, our words have authority and anointing. Guard our hearts and minds with the peace of Christ.

May we take up the shield of faith.
May we live by faith, as expressed by our trust in You, our reliance on You, our utter dependence on You. May we find in this faith safety and protection. Strengthen our faith-shields by revealing Yourself ever more clearly. Draw us into intimacy with You such that our vision of You is ever more clear, our knowledge of You ever deeper, and our resulting trust in You stronger and stronger.

Place in our hands the sword of the Spirit, which is the Word of God.
Grow in us a deep desire for Scripture, *because* it is YOUR Word. Quicken it to us. Through it, speak Your great love for us. May we allow Your holy Word to judge the thoughts and intentions of our hearts, piercing even to the innermost being. Teach us to be diligent to become skilled workmen who need not be ashamed, accurately handling Your Word. May the devil find us dangerous enemies by reason of the sword in our hands, which we wield to destroy his work. Bring Your Word to our minds exactly when and how it is needed.

Having been outfitted in Your armor, call us to battle.
Teach us to pray: with all prayer and petition may we pray at all times in the Spirit. Alert us to the needs of the saints and call us to persevere in prayer for those needs. Call us to pray open doors for the bold proclamation of the mystery of the gospel.

by Karen Smith, © 2006

COMPASS CHECK

- *How do you hear the voice of God? What does it sound like to you?*
- *How do you know when you are hearing the voice of the enemy?*
- *Put on the armor of God through prayer. You may wish to repeat this process regularly as you prepare to write your God Story.*

Chapter 6
The God Story Journal

Pilgrim Song
Unto you do I lift up my eyes,
O You Who are enthroned in heaven.
Behold, as the eyes of servants
look to the hand of their master,
and as the eyes of a maid
to the hand of her mistress,
so our eyes look to the Lord our God,
until he has mercy
and loving kindness for us.
Psalm 123:1-2 (AMP)

Overview

You are now ready to begin your God Story Journal. This is a process of looking back over your life story to discover where God was gently leading you and drawing you to Himself. As you explore your story, you will find that He was planting seeds and watering them along the way, telling you about who He is, about who you are, and about how eager He is to walk in an ever-deepening relationship with you.

It can be easy to think that in order to undertake this journey we need to muster a faith that is beyond ourselves. This is not true. Your availability and your willingness are essential offerings that God will use. This isn't a journey you are undertaking on your own, but one you are inviting God to join you in, asking Him to make up for what is lacking in your faith. In his book *The Pursuit of God,* A.W. Tozer includes a chapter titled, "The Gaze of the Soul." In it, the author reminds us that "believing… is directing the heart's attention to Jesus. It is lifting the mind to 'behold the Lamb of God,' and never ceasing that beholding for the rest of our lives. At first this may be difficult, but it becomes easier as we look steadily at His wondrous person, quietly and without strain. Distractions may hinder, but once the heart is committed to Him, after each brief excursion away from Him the attention will return again and rest upon Him like a wandering bird coming back to its window."

The discipline of remembering weaves together other spiritual disciplines: namely silence, solitude, prayer that listens (not just speaks), and fellowship. Pray that God will enable you to keep this a *spiritual* journey and not an *intellectual* pursuit. Pray for a willingness to be surprised by what the Spirit of God speaks to you. And pray that He will give you the confidence to pass on to others what you have learned about Him and what He has given you of Himself. To walk into your story is to find yourself in what really was, not what ought to have been. This can feel overwhelming; welcome the Holy Spirit's company as you begin this journey.

Logistics

You will need a place to write that is separate from your Devotional Journal. Carefully select the format which suits you best. Many people have enjoyed the flexibility provided by loose leaf paper in a three-ring binder; this allows the content of different writing Progressions (i.e. *What Have You Seen* and *What Have You Heard*) to be integrated into a single timeline, or for conversations re: forgotten passages of life to be integrated into the flow at a later date. However, you may find that you feel liberated to write freely by the borders of a bound journal and will develop other ways to add and annotate information. If you choose a journal you may want to write on every other page, leaving space for things remembered later. Choose whatever format feels like the right fit for you.

Set aside time to write your God Story. You will need to protect a solid chunk of time, preferably twice a week or more, in which you will be able to engage fully in this conversation with God. Choose a space with limited distractions that best facilitates this relational journey.

Keep in mind that your God Story is different from your daily Devotional Journal: in your Devotional Journal, you interact regularly with God regarding Scripture and your present life. In your God Story Journal, you will chronicle the events of your life in retrospect, looking for times where God was shaping your beliefs, getting your attention, and drawing you to Himself. As with the Devotional Journal, however, you should find a visual way to delineate between your voice and the voice of God as you write. You might use a red pen to signify the voice of God and a blue or black pen for your memories; this will make it easier to go back and read later. As described in Chapter 5, you will also hear the voice of the accuser as you write. You may wish to make note of his accusations in a third color of ink to clearly separate them from your conversation with the Father. This also allows you to observe patterns in the enemy's messages over the years and how he has sought to undermine your true identity and calling.

This writing is from you to God and from God to you. Don't worry about getting it right! There is no wrong way to do this, so long as you have set your heart on encountering God. Make it your own… even risk having fun doing it! Each person will walk through this process in a unique way. Your God Story is like no one else's. Take joy in its discovery.

EYES THAT SEE

In the Blockbuster film *The Matrix*, Morpheus offers Neo the choice to take the blue pill and remain oblivious to what is actually going on in the matrix of the world around him, or to take the red pill and see for himself what reality holds. As Neo considers his offer, Morpheus leans forward to make sure he understands: the Matrix isn't something that can be explained; it must be experienced with his own eyes. But he won't necessarily like what he sees. Neo's curiosity wins out, and he decides to step past the point of no return, swallowing the red pill.

If you are reading this, you have already decided to step back into the early parts of your story, examining the people and events that shaped you and asking God to meet you along the way. This choice to explore our God Stories is somewhat like taking the red pill: we suddenly emerge from our former understandings and perceptions of our lives and find ourselves looking back at our stories with new eyes.

In this shift, you may be tempted to let yourself become the focus, getting pulled down by the sheer weight of your story. However, this is an exercise both of stepping in to remember things from your unique story and of stepping back to ask God where He has been in your journey. We do not come to know God by knowing ourselves, but the exact opposite; we can only know ourselves as we come to know God. In the chapter previously mentioned, Tozer addresses the choice of letting God be the one upon whom our eyes gaze:

> I would emphasize this one committal, this one great volitional act which establishes the heart's intention to gaze forever upon Jesus. God takes this intention for our choice and makes what allowances He must for the thousand distractions which beset us in this evil world. He knows that we have set the direction of our hearts toward Jesus, and we can know it too, and comfort ourselves with the knowledge that a habit of soul is forming which will become after a while a sort of spiritual reflex requiring no more conscious effort on our part.

As you begin to think back on your story, ask God to give you eyes that see. First and foremost, this is a request to know the Author of your story in ways you otherwise could not. Ask Him to develop in you eyes of faith that can perceive His hand in the specific circumstances of your life. The purpose of having eyes that see will certainly extend much further than the redemption of your own story, but it must begin there. Remember that this vision will be unique to you; yet you are entering into a partnership with God that will help you see your story in the context of a much larger story that has been unfolding since the beginning of time. Consider Jesus' words, recorded in the book of John:

> All this I have spoken while still with you. But the Advocate, the Holy Spirit, whom the Father will send in my name, will teach you all things and will remind you of everything I have said to you. (John 14:25-26)

We can ask the Holy Spirit to teach us and remind us! He wants to do these things; He said He would. We can pray this for our lives as we journal through our God Story. After all, He has said *many things* to you and me personally. We are the ones who are called to ask, seek, knock, and keep on knocking (Luke 11:9).

Your choice to come to the feet of Jesus and invite Him to show you where He has been waiting to be discovered in your story is one that you should not take lightly. The God of the universe takes notice of your choice and is delighted by it. Don't let distractions convince you otherwise; rather, gently redirect your heart back to Him.

Looking back at our stories, we run the risk of becoming mired in fear, regret, hopelessness, or anger. For this reason, our goal must not be to figure our lives out. The discipline of remembering is intended to draw us into a new way of experiencing God. Again, Tozer speaks to this idea with clarity:

> Jesus taught that He wrought His works by always keeping His inward eyes upon His Father. His power lay in His continuous look at God (John 5:19-21)…. While we are looking at God we do not see ourselves—blessed riddance. The man who has struggled to purify himself and has had nothing but repeated failures will experience real relief when he stops tinkering with his soul and looks away to the perfect One. While he looks at Christ, the very things he has so long been trying to do will be getting done within him. It will be God working in him to will and to do.

In asking for eyes that see, we are asking for an increase in faith—first, to see God as we have not seen Him before, then to see ourselves in light of who God designed us to be, and finally to see our stories as part of a history that is unfolding and not beyond redemption, even as we live it.

Lord, it is so difficult—first to make the choice to want to see, and then to walk into the places where I haven't seen You. Be my Courage, my Strength, my Help, my Companion. There are places where I can't remember things, and this troubles me.

Would You please give me patience with myself, and the grace to journey at Your pace, not mine? Would You help me to see my stories with my heart, my soul, my mind, and my strength and in so doing to love You more, with all that I am? Teach me through this journey to trust You in ways I never would otherwise. And Lord, where I don't believe, would You help me to first see it, then admit it, and then to let You help me in my unbelief? You honored the man who spoke these words to You,(Mark 9:24) and I believe You have not changed. God, You are good—You are faithful—You are true.

Preparatory Postures

Begin your time with silence, becoming more present to yourself and to God who dwells in you. If you become distracted, don't berate yourself. Just choose to turn your heart again and again toward the One who is Love Himself. Ask God to reveal Himself to you as you remember and journal about your life. Believe that He hears your heart and will do just that.

You may want to begin your time with your hands upturned, eyes closed, picturing your hopes or fears for this time resting in your palms. Tell Jesus about what you hold in your hands. Ask Him to take your fears and replace them with the peace of His presence. As you welcome this peace, turn your palms over as a visible sign of your surrender. There is no hurry in this time; let your soul be anchored in the reality of His presence with you as you write.

Likewise, you may wish to place your hands on your chest and close your eyes, turning the eyes of your heart inward, centering your thoughts on where He is. He is not JUST in the universe around you; He is not JUST in the room with you; His dwelling is within you (Romans 5:1-4)—you are His temple (1 Corinthians 6:19). He is closer than the air around you (2 Timothy 1:13-14). When you do not sense Him, return to this place—to this posture—and wait for Him to speak.

Progession #1: What Have You Seen?

1. It is now time for you to begin your God Story Journal. You will write your life story, asking God where He has been at work and what He has done to awaken you to His presence. You may want to return to the questions and reflections from the Psalm 139 meditation in Chapter 2 as a launching point. Begin by asking God to take you back to your earliest memory. Explore your early recollections. Start at the beginning of your awareness as a child and take a look around. Write out everything you remember. Include specifics. Record what you hear God speaking to you about where He was, what He was doing, how He saw you, etc. Take as long as you need to discuss these early memories with God. Be creative in your thinking and your question asking.
   Example: When you were in your crib, what might have God been doing? As your mom was feeding or rocking you, what might He have been saying to her?

2. Move forward in roughly chronological order. You are writing an autobiography, looking for evidence of His presence as you remember. Keep in mind that this autobiography is not intended for a general audience. There is no need for it to be either perfect or presentable. Proper spelling and punctuation, for example, are unnecessary. As you return to it over time, feel free to fill in events you may have forgotten the first time around. A developing mosaic is more beneficial than an organized, sequential account.

Some things to keep in mind:

- You have seen and heard God in your life, even before you bowed your knee to His Lordship. He has been there all along, as in Hosea 11:3-4, inviting you to come to Him. This is the beginning of a long journey. Don't feel rushed. Take your time, walking into each new day of writing with an attitude of expectancy. Believe that God will meet you right where you are now. Wait and listen.

- In God's sovereignty, every situation—even the family in which He placed you (however godly or ungodly) has been covered by His loving purposes for you. Likewise, God will use every past experience to reveal Himself to you. Just begin to write your life story. You will see Him!

- The God Story journal is written in first person, dialogue form. If you're not sure that what you're hearing is actually what God has to say to you, then underline it to designate your uncertainty. One-on-one interaction with the Living God is the most important aspect of these exercises. Talk to Him. Ask Him to show you where He has been present in your life story and what He has spoken to you. He understands your uncertainty. This is new territory.

- You will develop *eyes that see* in the ordinary events of life. Where do you see His hand clearly evident in your past? Through what events has He invited you to join Him? Journal everything you see. Look for the smallest details. God is in them. Ask Him where, and take time to talk to Him about what He has done on your behalf. Offer up praise and worship for what you discover of His heart. Talk to God honestly; respond to Him when He reveals His presence in a place in your life. Give yourself permission to weep, sing, rejoice, lament, grieve, and praise.

- Return to the Psalm 139 meditation (Chapter 2) if you need ideas for questions, or ask God whatever questions come to mind. Take time to wait and hear His response, and then record it as a part of your God Story. Wander mentally through the days of your life—all the people, places, and things. Where did His name come up? Think of times when you felt very close to God and times when you felt far away. In times of pain, where was He? In times of joy, how was He rejoicing with you? How did He draw attention to Himself in the ways that were available to Him in your world?

- As you listen to your fellow sojourners share their stories, you will remember many things you had forgotten of your own story. Take notes along the way about further memories God may be inviting you to explore.

- Other members of your cohort may make their way through this writing process and arrive at the other Progressions slower or faster than you. There is no need to progress at a uniform pace.

Another excerpt from Patti's God Story Journal, to help you get started:
I remember the doll Granny gave me after I had my appendix removed. Even now the feelings come flooding back over me. The feelings of loving and being loved, nurturing and being nurtured. Funny those same feelings don't connect in my home; just with Granny. Lord, it was You who was awakening me to my longings, wasn't it?

Yes, Patti, that was Me. It was My love that you tasted from your Granny in those early years, touching your longings and awakening your thirst.

Salt-block events! You are amazing. Your Name doesn't have to be named for You to be present. You created my soul to long to be loved. You use small tastes of what You created me for to awaken those longings, to give me a taste of what You would give me later.

At that tender age, I was creating in you a hunger only I could fill. It would be years before you ceased assuming personal responsibility for satisfying that thirst and protecting yourself from the lack of satisfaction.

"When I told my story, you responded;
train me well in your deep wisdom.
Help me understand these things inside and out
so I can ponder your miracle-wonders.
My sad life's dilapidated, a falling-down barn;
build me up again by your Word.
Barricade the road that goes Nowhere;
grace me with your clear revelation.
I choose the true road to Somewhere,
I post your road signs at every curve and corner.
I grasp and cling to whatever you tell me;
God, don't let me down!
I'll run the course you lay out for me
if you'll just show me how."
(Psalm 119:26-32 The Message)

Chapter 7
Unveiling the Reflection

And we all, who with unveiled faces contemplate the Lord's glory, are being transformed into his image with ever-increasing glory, which comes from the Lord, who is the Spirit.
2 Corinthians 3:18

CREATED UNIQUENESS

An interesting focus will develop as you progress along this journey. As you listen to the stories of others, you will come to see in a very special way the uniqueness of each individual. Many of the stories will have things in common, yet God will be revealed through each person in ways you may never have seen. Each person truly reflects something unique of God's image.

When you woke up this morning, you had no way of knowing what you looked like until you paused in front of a mirror. This gave you an accurate representation of your external self. But that mirror could neither tell you about your soul nor about who you are on the inside.

When attempting to discern our true identities, we most often look in the mirror of other people's responses. If they smile at us, we feel good about ourselves. If they frown, we feel dejected. We may even wonder if something is wrong with us. These responses include people's verbal messages about us. When you learn that someone has said something about you, do you ever want to find out what they said? We all do! We listen to find out who we are. Each of us seeks to piece together a clear picture of what we have to offer that those around us might enjoy.

Distorted Mirrors

The problem with finding our identities in the mirror of other people's approval is that these mirrors, shaped by sin and forged in a fallen world, do not reveal our true reflection. Instead, each person gives us a distorted view of ourselves, like so many distorted mirrors at a carnival. Standing in front of a warped mirror, you might find that your feet have grown to a size 30, your legs have shrunk by eighteen inches, and your mid-section has widened by twelve sizes. Would you then go home and alter your wardrobe? Of course not! But each of us has adjusted our self-perception, along with our behaviors and habits, to fit the skewed mirror of another person's responses.

I grew up with a mother who, for whatever reason, had cut off many of her emotional responses to the world around her and therefore gave very little of herself. As the first-born, I initially gleaned what little attention she had to offer. However, once my brother came along twenty-one months later, I had to share this thin portion of affection. In my child's mind, I experienced the loss of her relationship as a personal rejection and came to believe that my brother was much more loveable than myself. Over time, this conviction grew, extending beyond familial borders to overshadow all other relationships. I was convinced that any friendship I had was automatically undermined by the addition of a third person, as my original friend would clearly prefer the new person to myself. My pattern was to reflexively withdraw from any friendship that embraced a third person.

Two falsehoods are apparent in my childhood perception. The first was that my mother's response had anything to do with my true identity. In fact, her style of relating had everything to do with her own inability (or unwillingness) to love well. The second falsehood was in the reflection I then extended to my friends. Feeling unwanted when a third person entered a friendship, I would begin to avoid my initial friend. Depending on that friend's own beliefs and experiences, she might take my distance to mean any number of things about herself.

Do you see why it is so risky to look to others for our sense of identity? The many voices around you may say that you have value if you drive a nice car, wear a certain brand of clothing, look attractive, perform well as an athlete, or speak intelligently. These messages change constantly and vary based on your setting. Some come from media and advertising sources while others are communicated directly by the people closest to you. This can lead to a great confusion about who you are.

If we don't measure up to the standards of those around us, we usually look for some other way to gain the love and respect our hearts were created to enjoy. At the same time, we might find ways to protect ourselves from the pain of rejection by developing defensive strategies, thus becoming our own fortresses of safety.

The Wrapped Box

This way of hiding is much like crawling into a box and then decorating the box to best please the people at hand. We have the illusion that we can keep others from seeing us as we see ourselves or feeling about us as we do. We watch the responses of others to discover what they want of us: would they prefer the soccer-themed gift wrap? How about something chic and sophisticated? Perhaps plain, brown paper would be best. All the while we are asking, "Can you love me now?" We go to these lengths because we really don't believe that anyone would like what they saw if we were to open the box. We don't think that we like what is in the box, either; we have believed the messages of all those warped mirrors. Our awareness of our own sin gives us further reason to feel uncertain about whether we have anything good to offer.

The only mirror we can gaze upon to see a true picture of ourselves is the mirror of God's perfect love. His Word, His Spirit, and the death of His Son for us on the cross combine to give a true representation of how He sees us (see Romans 5:1-5).

Let's take a look inside the box to consider what exactly God sees when He looks at you. He doesn't even need to unwrap the box to recognize you as the handcrafted, one-of-a-kind Waterford crystal goblet that He lovingly fashioned. Most of us, comparing ourselves to others, come up short. We don't believe what God says about us. We figure that we are probably a common water glass at best, or we might feel like Styrofoam cups most of the time. Yet God carefully designed each of us so that His glory would shine through! Now, when God holds up your piece of crystal, is it chipped, cracked and smudged because of your sin against Him and others and the sin of other people against you? Of course it is! But those flaws are not yours to fix—in fact, you can't do anything about them! They are the reason Jesus Christ died and rose again for you. 'While we were yet chipped and cracked and smudged, Christ died for us' (Romans 5:8, author's paraphrase).

Ephesians 1:4 reveals that you were fashioned in the mind of the living God before the foundation of the world. Isaiah 43:1, 4, 6-7, and 21 declare that the purpose of your existence is for God's glory, pleasure and enjoyment. Malachi 3:17 says that you are His special treasure, and Psalm 139 proclaims that He carefully formed the person you would become while you were yet in your mother's womb. He made no mistakes with you. He even counted how many hairs would be on your head. You are very special to God. *All the factors that have come together to make you who you are have never before existed on the face of the earth, nor ever will again. You are very loved and very unique. You are His handiwork.* He created you first and foremost for His own enjoyment and glory, and He wants you to enjoy His handiwork in you as well—to enjoy being who He made you to be. He also wants those around you to richly enjoy His handiwork.

Every morning when I get up, one of the first things I do is look at the mountains. They cause my heart to sing God's praises. And they are only mountains! If I am drawn to praise Him over the majesty of inanimate objects, how much greater should be my praise when I look at you and see His image? C.S. Lewis says that if we could see each other as we will exist in Glory, we would be tempted to bow down and worship each other. That is the glory of bearing the divine image. When we hide ourselves, we are hiding God's image that we bear. If we refuse to freely offer who we are to those around us, we are depriving them of the opportunity to experience our singular reflection of Him; we leave a hole in the place we were designed to fill.

> For our light, momentary affliction (this slight distress of the passing hour) is ever more and more abundantly preparing and producing and achieving for us an everlasting weight of glory, [beyond all measure, excessively surpassing all comparisons and all calculations, a vast and transcendent glory and blessedness never to cease!] (2 Corinthians 4:17 AMP)

Some years ago, my youngest son Wes, a musician, went through a time where he felt despondent about what he had to offer musically. He wanted to know why he couldn't be like Chopin. Or like his friend Kelvin, who could play anything well and without any effort at all. Truly, Wes didn't play like Chopin or like Kelvin. God had not created Wes to reveal to the world what Chopin or Kelvin were created to reveal. If Wes tried to imitate these other men, or gave up hope because he was gifted in some other way, then the rest of us would never know what we were supposed to learn about God through Wes.

Consider Revelation 2:17:

> Whoever has ears, let them hear what the Spirit says to the churches. To the one who is victorious, I will give some of the hidden manna. I will also give that person a white stone with a new name written on it, known only to the one who receives it.

I believe that the name given to you will be directly linked to who you are to God, what He has given you to bear of His image, and the way He has chosen to go about refining and purifying you.

Have you ever caught sight of the sunset in your rearview mirror and turned to see the whole view? When you are willing to be whatever God has created you to be, people catch in your likeness a glimpse of the Creator. They turn to see Who it is you reflect, and their eyes are drawn to Him. His gaze awaits them, looking intently toward them to capture their hearts.

"For the god of this world has blinded the unbelievers' minds [that they should not discern the truth], preventing them from seeing the illuminating light of the Gospel of the glory of Christ (the Messiah), Who is the Image and Likeness of God. For what we preach is not ourselves but Jesus Christ as Lord, and ourselves [merely] as your servants (slaves) for Jesus' sake. For God Who said, Let light shine out of darkness, has shone in our hearts so as [to beam forth]

the Light for the illumination of the knowledge of the majesty and glory of God [as it is manifest in the Person and is revealed] in the face of Jesus Christ (the Messiah). However, we possess this precious treasure [the divine Light of the Gospel] in [frail, human] vessels of earth, that the grandeur and exceeding greatness of the power may be shown to be from God and not from ourselves." (II Corinthians 4:4-7 AMP)

EARS THAT HEAR

You have traveled through Progression #1, reliving your life's journey and considering what you have *seen* of God along the way. I am sure you have found that God was there long before you thought to look for Him. He has been there at every moment of your life, showing you something of Himself. During this time, He has not been silent. You will now begin to journal about what you have *heard*. God has used the things present in your life to speak to you—to touch your heart and draw your attention to Himself. What are the audible, linguistic, musical and literary ways you have heard the voice of God?

This next winding passageway on the Journey to Remembering is an exploration of the specific words through which God has revealed Himself to you. You will consider the words of life that have woven their way through your narrative, annotating them chronologically into your God Story Journal in the places they arose and wherever you recall them re-emerging. You will also interact with God about them in journal form. You may either choose to designate a new section of your God Story journal for this Progression or simply add these pages of writing into the timeline of what you have already written. Choose the format which best helps you to stay engaged at a heart level and in the flow of relational conversation with God. Ask God why He gave you these particular truths. Why did He use these words and not others? He is purposeful in His speaking. You are an arrow, fashioned by the hand of your Creator and designed by Him to accomplish His specific purpose. The ideas He has spoken to you will help in revealing that purpose.

Progession #2: What Have You Heard?

1) As with the first Progression, you will start by looking back to your earliest memories and work forward from there. As you do so, search for messages you encountered which were in fact God's words specifically for you. Perhaps these came in the form of encouraging words spoken to you, a poem, a song you heard, books by a favorite author, or a passage of Scripture that resonated deeply. Mine your life for truths that were made uniquely yours. As you write these words down, you may feel tempted to engage with them in an intellectual way. Instead, ponder them in your heart and focus on interacting with God about them. Cherish the reality that He has used any and all ways available to speak to you. Thank Him for how these ideas guided you toward true life. Ask Him how He wishes you to continue applying these truths and what they communicate about your calling.

1) Consider the first "word of life" that you recall. Write it down. Meditate on it. Consider when in your narrative it first emerged. Ask God what He was telling you and why He said it at that moment. Talk to God about what you love in this message and how it has led you toward Him. Ask Him why He gave it to you and what He has done and continues to do through its presence in your life. Repeat this process with other messages you heard that burned within you over the years.

2) Some of what you have heard could be treasured portions of Scripture. Keep in mind that while we often perceive ourselves as the ones who have discovered valuable verses in the Bible, God has in fact personally whispered those verses to us for a specific purpose. The fact that it ever leapt to your awareness was an act of the Holy Spirit. In addition, consider verses you may have memorized because of their special meaning to you. What was God teaching you about Himself through these verses? How was He casting your future?

3) The truth of the Word of God has had an impact on your life through many avenues. Think back on times when truth from a sermon, radio message, song, conversation, personal testimony of another believer, etc. had an impact in your life. What did God teach you in that situation about Himself, His Word, His Spirit, His love, His plan for your life? As you rehearse what

He has said to you through these many avenues, you will begin to see a personal Life Message unfold. Your Life Message is about your relationship with Him. What is it? Write it down.

4) After you have traversed these pathways of biblical truth in your life, jot down any themes which have emerged. How are these truths personally yours? How have they impacted your life?

5) Ask God how He wants you to pass on to others what He has uniquely revealed to you.

6) Allow this Progression to take as much time as is required to engage with the messages of truth God has spoken into your life across the span of your years, experiences and relationships. There is no hurry to complete this Progression. Allow it to unfold, and wait on God as He discloses Himself and His words to you.

Chapter 8
Exploring God's Love

And so we know and rely on the love God has for us.
God is love. Whoever lives in love lives in God, and God in them.
1 John 4:16

CONVERSATIONS *WITH* GOD

Most of us as Christians have been invited into many conversations about God. I, for one, have loved nothing more than to enter conversation with other students of God's Word to share insights, observations, questions, and convictions. Those conversations have strengthened my faith and encouraged me along the path suggested by II Timothy 2:15: "Do your best to present yourself to God as one approved, a worker who does not need to be ashamed and who correctly handles the word of truth."

Since the Reformation and the invention of the printing press, we have come a very long way in increasing knowledge about God and His Word. Too often, we have equated the knowledge of truth with faith itself. However, the fact that I know something does not mean that I actually believe. Belief is measured by conviction; conviction is measured by my willingness to lay down my life for what I believe.

Often have I grieved before God because of my inability to trust Him, my sin against Him, my coldness of heart, my lack of any consistent engagement of my heart with His. In John 4, Jesus tells the woman at the well that if she knew Who she was talking to she would ask…and He would give. Jesus tells her that the Father's desire is for those who worship Him to worship Him in spirit and in truth. This woman was in conversation with the living God—she asked Him questions, and He asked questions of her. She gave Him information, and He gave information to her. He touched her heart deeply because in effect He said to her, "Daughter, what I say of Myself in Psalm 139 is true for My relationship with you. I have been in your life all along. There has not been a moment when I was not there. I was there through the pain of five husbands and I have been there in the relationship you are in now." Does this sound like a God Story reading to you? *"If you knew who you are talking to you would ask..."*

There is a significant difference between a community that has conversations *about* God and a community that has conversations *with* God. I noticed this in the pilot study when we moved from the *What Have You Seen?* and *What Have You*

Heard? Progressions to the *God is the Lover of Your Soul* segment. We approached the latter as a study and discussed what we saw about God in the verses and how they touched our hearts. In contrast to the previous weeks, we realized that something was very different. The whole tone of our time together had changed. We were no longer listening in on a conversation with God; rather, we were dialoguing amongst ourselves about God. The difference was palpable. We decided to adjust: we would talk to God about the verses and listen for what He wanted to say in response. We would journal the conversation and then come together to read it aloud and invite each other to listen in. What a difference this made! Clearly, there is a place for conversation about God—don't get me wrong. However, it is no substitute for conversation *with* God and the communion that occurs between Father, Son, Holy Spirit and the community of believers when we share these conversations with each other.

What the Bible is Saying

The first time I did the following Bible study was in the summer of 1970. I was overwhelmed. I had no idea how God saw me or what His love was like. The study *God is the Lover of My Soul*, originally titled *God Loves Me*, was written by Ruth Denler Myers. The Lord put it in my hands in the summer of 1970. I have done this study countless times with both groups and individuals. Not only has this study changed my life and my entire understanding of God, it has guided the direction my life has taken. I will be eternally grateful to Ruth Myers, although I have only spoken with her by phone. When I first delved into this study, I began to pray (and have prayed countless times since) that God would grant me the privilege of extending His arms to those around me to invite them to come sit at His feet and fall more deeply in love with Him, coming to understand at a much deeper level how much He loves them as individuals. He has answered this prayer through the intimacy of shared conversation.

Do you truly believe that the Living God is the Lover of your soul? Do you allow the fact that God loves you to affect your responses to Him? Does the reality of His love impact how you feel and your reactions to circumstances and people? This knowledge should affect every facet of your life! The words "love," "affection," and "devotion" all equate to "a deep and enduring emotional regard, usually for another person." These refer to strong personal attachment, with ardent care, which includes sympathetic understanding, good will, and benevolent action, as well as a delight and pleasure in the loved one.

God's love for you is all this and more. It defies human definition. The only way you can know God's love for you is by allowing the Holy Spirit to teach you to make the love messages He has given in the Scriptures your own in daily experience.

We are choosing not to approach *God is the Lover of My Soul* in a classic study format. Whenever possible, the questions here have been re-worded from the traditional third-person point of view into a first-person conversational format. As such, questions will most often be phrased as though they were spoken from your perspective and addressed either to yourself or to the triune God. Sometimes they will be directed specifically to the Father, Son, or Holy Spirit. Your task is to converse with God about the questions and verses found here and record these conversations in your God Story Journal. Again, make Eph. 3:19-21 your prayer as you journal and prayerfully meditate upon the following questions and Scriptures:

> [That you may really come] to know [practically, through experience for yourselves] the love of Christ, which far surpasses mere knowledge [without experience]; that you may be filled [through all your being] unto all the fullness of God [may have the richest measure of the divine Presence, and become a body wholly filled and flooded with God Himself]! Now to Him Who, by (in consequence of) the [action of His] power that is at work within us, is able to [carry out His purpose and] do superabundantly, far over and above all that we [dare] ask or think [infinitely beyond our highest prayers, desires, thoughts, hopes, or dreams] – To Him be glory in the church and in Christ Jesus throughout all generations forever and ever. Amen (so be it). (AMP)

As you proceed through this leg of the journey, the writing and session formats will remain the same. There will be no group discussion of this time spent studying God's word—the focus will remain on what God is saying to each person. We will continue to listen in on the conversations taking place between the triune God and our fellow sojourners. As you progress through this passageway, take your time. Don't rush! Consider it a beautiful vista full of new discoveries. Focus on gaining a deeper understanding of God, identifying where He has been in your life, unearthing how He feels about you, and understanding how He wants you to feel about Him.

Go back and review the questioning and reflection format used with Psalm 139 in Chapter 2. Then look up the verses, one at a time, and begin to ask God questions about what you read. Wait and listen. He will speak. By now you have grown in your confidence that He does in fact want to speak personally to you.

Progession #3: GOD Is The Lover Of My Soul, Part I

1. To begin, read through the following samples of my conversation with God regarding Psalm 13:5-6 and Psalm 63, each of which took place during different seasons in my life. Then consider these passages of Scripture for yourself and journal through your interaction with God about them. As you will see, He may say different things to the same person at different times, or different things about the same passage to different people. I wish I could be there to listen in on your conversation with Him so that I could see Him through your eyes and gaze on the piece of His image that you reflect.

> **But I have trusted, leaned on, and been confident in Your mercy and loving-kindness; my heart shall rejoice and be in high spirits in Your salvation. I will sing to You Lord, because You have dealt bountifully with me. (Psalm 13:5-6 AMP)**

> Oh Lord, what goes on in Your heart when I speak these words to You? What goes on in Your heart when I sing to You because of the bountiful way You have dealt with me? **Child, I am glorified when you recognize My love for you. Your natural response to My love is worship. In that moment, you and I are in perfect communion – I loving, you worshipping. For this did I create.**
> Abba, have I trusted You? Have I leaned on You? Has my confidence been in Your mercy and loving-kindness? Do I even understand the concepts of mercy and loving-kindness? I know that I have studied them, but do I really understand them? Do I live as if Your love is kind and merciful, or do I live as if I need to take care of myself because You might not take care of me the way I want to be taken care of? **Child, how would *you* answer this?** At times I fear, I fear exposure and rejection, I pull back from those You have sent me to. **What does pulling back protect you from, Patti?** The pain of not been wanted, of being seen the way my parents saw me, the way others have seen me. **How much of what they saw was true?** A good bit. **How much was not true, how much of what you fear others might see came from the lies the hater spoke into your heart?** That is the question, isn't it? Who do I trust? It seems safer to trust the hater. Then I can protect myself from the disappointment of others when I carelessly wound them or do not love well.

Patti, why would you choose to believe the hater? What does that have to do with your understanding of My mercy and loving kindness? Do you believe I am kind and loving when others are disappointed in you for legitimate or illegitimate reasons? Or do you believe the hater? It isn't about belief; it is about control. **So I am kind and merciful, but in My kindness and mercy I am in control of what comes to you—you are not.** Yes Lord, that is true. **What do you want to do with that, Patti?** Well I certainly don't want to give the enemy the territory by trusting *him* to protect me. **Yes?** Then I need to walk into what You have set before me, believing and acting on that belief that You are merciful – You do not deal with me according to my iniquities. And You do not set anything before me that leaves me alone. You are there. **Does that cause you to sing, child? What happens to your heart when you find Me in a painful circumstance?** I want to stay there, and I beg You to ignore my cries for relief. **Yes, so sing to Me from that place and you will understand My kindness and My mercy more deeply.** Thank You, Abba.

What makes the Psalmist say that his heart shall rejoice and be in high spirits in Your salvation? What is it about this man's relationship with You that enables him to see You clearly this way? He sings to You. That assumes that You desire him to sing to You.
Of course I do. Child, you have watched many movies where the lover sings of his love for the one he loves. Why should I be different? Do you remember Zephaniah 3:17 where I talk of exulting over you with singing? Why would I not want that equally from you? I am relational. Remember, I want to have the same relationship with you that I have with the Son and the Spirit. Remember what Jesus said about us in John 17. He revealed Us to you perfectly. Do you see Jesus abiding alone, isolated, not noticing when someone moves toward Him or cares for Him? No, He is completely involved in relationship with His friends. He called them friends, and He invited them into an abiding relationship in John 15. They are so important to Him that He lays down His life to have them for His own. Think about the things He is saying about Us. We call you friend, child. We want your joy in Us to be full (John 15) and abundant (John 10). Joy brings singing. That is amazing, Lord.

Psalm 63:3 O GOD, You are my God, earnestly will I seek You; my inner self thirsts for You, my flesh longs and is faint for You, in a dry and weary land where no water is. So I have looked upon You in the sanctuary to see Your power and Your glory. Because Your loving-kindness is better than life, my lips shall praise You.

Abba, the wisdom in these verses stuns me. You call me to seek You, to earnestly seek You; to put my whole being into seeking for You. You have placed a thirst in my inner being that can only be satisfied by You. Even my physical being is affected by Your absence. I faint outwardly because of the inner thirst. I love this; it is the same as Psalm 73—the psalmist went to Your Sanctuary. To the place he knew You could be found. He knew that was the only place water for his soul could be found. In my thirst and longing I have looked on You, Father. My thirst has driven me to look upon You in Your sanctuary—Your holy place. Your glory and power are evident there, and there I am stunned by Your loving-kindness. It becomes better than life itself to me. You even draw me to look at You because You love me and are kind toward me. And where do I find Your Sanctuary? It is within me. I need only look inward to find You where You have taken up residence.

Child, I always hide within the pages of My letter to you the secret of your inner thirst. I never leave you wondering where to find Me, and I never leave you wondering what you thirst for. Oh yes, the hater of your soul has certainly drawn you off from the Sanctuary, but always your thirst increases after a foray with him. And child, your soul again returns to Me as a bird to its window. Dear one, remember to look at Me, behold Me as in a glass. What could you possibly find that would compare to Me, that could satisfy your thirst and your longing? You are My Sanctuary, you are My Temple. Place your hands on your heart, Patti, and turn your eyes to where I am to be found.

2. Meditate on the following verses, one at a time, and write a dialogue with God about them in your God Story journal. Write out your questions and God's answers as well as His questions and your answers. Journal through the whole conversation that these verses inspire between you and God:
   Psalm 103:11
   Psalm 108:4
   Psalm 136:1
   Isaiah 63:7
   I John 4:7
   Psalm 36:7
   Psalm 86:5
   Psalm 103:17
   Song of Songs 1:4
   I John 3:1-2
   I John 4:18

3. Father, according to Isaiah 54:10, what is the quality and duration of Your love for me? Because Hebrews 13:8 is true of You, what is likewise true of Your love and all Your other attributes?

4. On the basis of what You have revealed to me from the preceding verses, when did Your love for me begin? When will Your love for me end? Could it be mine because I deserved it? Will it ever fluctuate or lessen?

5. From the previous verses, write out the words and phrases you like best to describe God's love. Interact with God about the various qualities of His love for you as found in the following verses:
   Psalm 145:8-9
   II Samuel 22:36
   Psalm 103:8
   Isaiah 63:7, 9

6. Another heartwarming aspect of Your love is Your *desire* for me. How do the following verses help me to comprehend the fact that You desire me?
   Ephesians 1:4
   John 4:23
   Song of Songs 2:10, 14; 7:10

7. Your desire for me is also shown in Your longing for an intimate relationship with me. What have You done for me that reveals this longing?
   Exodus 19:4
   Hosea 11:3, 4
   Jeremiah 31:3

"I have loved you with an everlasting love; I have drawn you with unfailing kindness" (Jeremiah 31:3).
Patti, I have loved you with a love that has no end and no beginning; because of this love I have kindly drawn you. Yes Lord, You have been kind, so kind. Kindness was not something offered in my home. You knew I needed that. I liken myself to a feral cat; You knew that and acted accordingly. And everlasting love—there has never been a time when You did not love me! I am still learning to wrap my mind around that. I have come to understand it as I allow the knowledge to sink in, listening to You say it over and over. It gives me the courage to trust You in every circumstance. **Child, has there ever been a time when I did not love you? You have just held David, your third grandchild. Can you see how vulnerable he is? Are you aware of how little he knows or understands? You are in My arms in that same way. Little David's thoughts are not your thoughts and his ways are not your ways. He has no comprehension of the world around him; he must be totally dependent on your thoughts and ways. I know that you can no more understand the world you are in than David can, and I grieve that you are outside the Garden. But if you, being evil, know how to care for this small infant, how much more I, your Father in Heaven.** But Lord, David is innocent. I ran from You. I sinned against You when I knew the truth about You. How could You love me when I ran from You? When I danced with Your enemy? Were You not disgusted with me? **Disgusted with you? Child, My righteous anger burned white hot against My Son for your sin. I hate sin – it is a fist in My face. But Patti, I love you more than I hate sin. But My righteous anger had to be faced and satisfied. I could not deny My Holiness, and I could not deny My love for you. That left Me only one alternative: give My Son for you. And so I did.**

> **How could I love you when you ran from Me, when you danced with My enemy? Do you have any idea the grief I felt when you ran, the sorrow at seeing the one who hates you drawing you into his web? Though I know that I will in the end prevail, I hate the wounds and scars he is able to inflict on you when you yield to his lies. The wounds that fell on you fell on Me.**

8. How near to Yourself have You brought me?
   Galatians 2:20
   II Corinthians 6:16

9. What specific relationships demonstrate how near and dear I am to You?
   I John 3:1
   Isaiah 62:5
   Romans 8:15
   II Corinthians 11:2

10. What do You say I mean to You in Isaiah 43:4 and Ephesians 1:1-18?

11. According to Daniel 10:19 and Colossians 3:12, what am I like in Your eyes?

12. What amazing fact about Your love for me as my Father is shown in John 17:23 and Ephesians 1:6?

13. According to John 15:9, how do You love me, Jesus?

> Are you finding conversing with God through His word exciting? Don't let yourself slide. Keep asking and listening and recording. It only gets better!

14. How a person feels about another is shown in his actions. How did You most fully reveal the degree of Your love for me?
    John 3:16, 15:13
    Romans 5:8

Have you responded to His love by completely giving yourself to Him?

Just as I am, without one plea
But that Thy blood was shed for me,
And that Thou bid'st me come to Thee,
O Lamb of God, I come.
Just as I am, Thy love, unknown
Has broken every barrier down,
Now to be Thine, yes, Thine alone
O Lamb of God, I come.
-- Charlotte Elliott

God, in His quest to demonstrate His love, does not seek people with imposing lists of humanly desired qualities, nor is His love reserved for a limited number of "successful" Christians. Because He is love and because He created me for Himself and bought me to be His own, He loves me and always will.

11. From I Corinthians 1:26-29, what do I learn about why You chose me and set Your love upon me? How does this contrast with why I might expect a great King to desire me? According to Deuteronomy 7:6 and Jeremiah 9:23-24, do my human advantages and attainments impress You?

12. As stated in Romans 5:6,8,10, what was I like when You showed Your love by dying for me?

13. According to Psalm 40:11-13, 17, to whom do You demonstrate Your loving-kindness? Do I qualify?

14. Your love and grace are inseparably intertwined. What is grace? What does this reveal about the basis on which I can expect to experience Your love? Is Your love something I gain by successful performance?
    Romans 11:6
    Ephesians 2:8-9
    Colossians 2:6

> Thinking on a loved one's words helps cement an intimate relationship. Which of the verses in this meditation helps you most to sense God's love? What can you do to assure that you will think on this verse often?

15. God has shown His love in many ways. Journal about the verses or phrases that stand out to you in the following list:

God, Your love is shown…

• In Your good plan for me	Psalm 40:5 Isaiah 25:1 Jeremiah 29:11
• In the reasons You want me to obey You:	Deut. 5:29 Isaiah 48:17-18 Proverbs 1:33 Joshua 1:8
• In Your gracious providing and giving:	Romans 8:32 Hosea 2:8 II Corinthians 8:9
• In what You take away or withhold:	Hosea 2:6-9 Psalm 84:11 Jeremiah 5:25
• In Your protecting of me:	Deut. 33:12, 17 Isaiah 25:4, 43:2 Psalm 12:1
• In Your desire to improve and beautify my life:	Isaiah 54:11-12, 61:10 Ephesians 5:27
• In Your chastening:	Hebrews 12:6 Lamentations 3:31-33
• In Your attentiveness to me:	Psalm 33:12, 14, 18 Psalm 34:15 Matthew 10:29-31

- In Your desire to communicate with me: Proverbs 2:1-2
Proverbs 22:17-18
Song of Songs 2:10
- In Your desire for my unrivaled love: Deuteronomy 6:5
Exodus 34:14
- In Your constant acceptance and welcome: Ephesians 3:12
Ephesians 1:6
Hebrews 4:16
- In Your attitude even when I sin: Isaiah 44:22
Luke 15:20-24
Hosea 3:1
Romans 4:8, 8:33-39
- In Your forgiving and forgetting: Psalm 103:11-14
Proverbs 10:12
Hebrews 8:12

"Satisfy us in the morning with your unfailing love, that we may sing for joy and be glad all our days." (Psalm 90:14)

Progession #4: GOD Is The Lover Of My Soul, Part II
The following was originally Ruth Myer's Bible study *How Can I Enjoy His Love More.* Although it is a study, we are choosing again not to use that format. Your mission is to converse with God about the questions and verses found here and record your conversations in your God Story Journal. You may return to Progression #3 to review the instructions.

Again, review the questioning and reflection format of the Psalm 139 meditation in chapter 2. Begin to ask God questions about the following verses. Recognize that He is speaking to you through them. Consider what He is saying to you. Wait and listen.

And I ask him that with both feet planted firmly on love, you'll be able to take in with all followers of Jesus the extravagant dimensions of Christ's love. Reach out and experience the breadth! Test its length! Plumb the depths! Rise to the heights! Live full lives, full in the fullness of God.
(Ephesians 3:17-19 The Message)

The Bible gives many instructions that can guide us in our lifelong adventure of exploring His limitless love. Various men in Scripture pursued God with all their hearts and experienced a loving, intimate relationship with Him. Others only wanted His benefits in times of obvious need but cared little about Him as a Person. God does not force His love onto indifferent hearts. He wants us to seek Him wholeheartedly and to receive of His love consistently.

1. David was called a man after Your own heart. What was his dominant interest and desire?
   Psalm 41:1-2
   Psalm 27:4
   Psalm 17:15

2. Of all of Jesus' disciples, John speaks most of His love. What three verbs did John use in I John 4:16 to show what the Lord wants me to do about His love?

3. What fact is always the starting point for a deeper love for You? From beginning to end in my relationship with You, which one of us courts and wins love?

4. In Song of Songs 2:10, 14 what do You, the initiator in our love relationship, desire of me? What further light does Psalm 27:8 shed on how You want me to respond?

5. What did David and Moses ask You to do regarding Your love, and when?
   Psalm 143:8
   Psalm 90:14
   How should this, along with the answer to Question 4, affect the way I begin my days?

6. According to the following examples, what other times are good for seeking You and enjoying Your loving presence?
   Song of Songs 1:7
   Psalm 63:5-8

   Note also Song of Songs 2:3. When might a shepherd girl delight to find shade and refreshing fruit? This is the same for me when I need Your love.

7. Why is it important for me to meditate on Your love as recorded in Scripture rather than merely on my thoughts about Your love?
   I Thessalonians 2:13
   Hebrews 4:12

8. The better I know what You, my Beloved, are like, the more I will value Your love and respond to it. Seeing the beauty of Your character, Your strength, Your victories, Your positions, and Your attitudes can fill me with awe that You love me. Which descriptive phrases in the following verses most help me to adore You and respond to Your desire for intimate fellowship with me?
   Psalm 145:1-13
   Colossians 1:15-19
   Psalm 104:1-3
   Psalm 113:2-6
   Psalm 68:32-34
   Ephesians 1:19-21
   Psalm 45:1-9
   Hebrews 1:23

9. Like rays emanating from the sun, love is always shining from Your heart. But I can turn my back to You and experience night instead of light. According to Psalm 66:18, what can prevent communication between You and me?

   In Isaiah 59:1-2, You spoke to Your people about specific sins. They refused to repent. As a result, what did their sins and iniquities do?

10. If I feel that something is blocking out the warmth of Your love like a dark cloud, what should I ask You to do as I come to Your Word?
    Psalm 139:23
    Hebrews 4:12-13

> Remember that a vague sense of condemnation is not from God. He never condemns His children, and He is always specific in revealing sin. Remember also that sin in God's sight is not just our stereotyped "dos and don'ts." It includes pride, self-will, self-reliance, uncommitted dreams and ambitions, and such attitudes as indifference, hostility, anxiety, self-condemnation, unbelief—even the sin of not believing that He has forgiven me after I confess!

11. When the prodigal son returns to his father in Luke 15:20, what does his father do (even before the son verbally confesses)?

    In Luke 15:22-24, immediately after the son's confession what does the father say?

    Is a period of probation necessary to prove the son's "worthiness"?

12. Likewise, in Hosea 14:1-4, what does the Lord promise those who honestly confess their sins and turn to Him?

13. What do You desire in my heart response and in my actions so that You can increasingly demonstrate Your love and presence to me?
    John 14:21
    Deuteronomy 7:9

14. Jesus, what is the source of the love and obedience of which You spoke in Philippians 2:13?

According to I John 5:4-5, what is my part that assures obedient, victorious living?

According to Hebrews 12:2, what is the source of my faith?

Do I in any way earn Your love by my ability to believe and obey?

> God's love draws me to dedicate myself to love Him above all and to do His will. Dedication draws me to the place where His love shines most clearly. Walking the path of obedience does not mean I earn His love. It merely means I choose the highway where the glory of His love shines undimmed, in preference to the dark paths that I grope along when I forget His love and try to get my needs met my own way.

15. Holy Spirit, according to Romans 5:5, what is one ministry You perform in my life?
    What must I let You do within me so I can know the Father's love (Ephesians 3:16-19)?
    [Notice how often the indwelling presence of Christ through the Holy Spirit is connected to love.]
    John 14:23, 15:5-9
    Galatians 2:20, 5:14-16, 22
    I John 4:11-12, 3:16

> Because God's Holy Spirit dwells within me, my experience of His love can intimately surpass any human love relationship. He is love. As I let Him control my mind, emotions, and will, and believe Him to fill and permeate my inner being, I am filled with love.

16. Relying on Your love within me, what commandment must I especially obey if I desire to continue abiding in Your love?
    I John 4:11-12
    John 15:12, 13:34
    Galatians 5:14

17. What does I John 4:20-5:2 say about the relationship between love for You and love on the human level?

> If I let hostility toward another person block the outflow of love from my life, the inner flow of God's love is hindered. The feeling against the other person obstructs my whole life. Keeping short accounts with others as well as with God is essential.

18. Father, according to Romans 5:3-4, what do You allow to happen in my life so that the Holy Spirit will enable me to be more aware of how dearly You love me?

    Therefore, what attitudes toward difficulties should I have if I want to cooperate with You and expedite Your work?

    Romans 5:3
    Hebrews 12:5-7, 12-13

19. "Every joy or trial falleth from above, traced upon our dial by the Sun of Love" (from the hymn, <u>Like A River Glorious</u>). What do Your love gifts reveal about Your perspective on my enjoyment of life? How can I be sure that the good things You send will deepen our love relationship?

    I Timothy 6:17b
    Psalm 10:1-5
    Hosea 2:8, 13-16

> Praise keeps God central in both my enjoyments and my trials, making Him the focal point of my life.

20. According to Psalm 33:22, the degree to which I experience Your love is determined by the degree to which my hope is *in* You.

    Psalm 62:5

    Comparing Psalm 147:11 and I John 4:18, what will my attitude toward You and the future be as I become more convinced that You truly love me?

A satisfying love relationship with God, as with anyone, demands time and teamwork. It must be cultivated, often at the cost of eliminating some seemingly important personal interests that are of lesser value. A casual, lukewarm, haphazard approach to Him will not suffice. It has been said that we get out of life that which we truly want. How seriously do you want to know God's love? Are there areas of life in which you are holding Him at arm's length so He cannot demonstrate His love and desire for you?

Chapter 9
Thirst

"You, God, are my God, earnestly I seek you; I thirst for you, my whole being longs for you, in a dry and parched land where there is no water."
Psalm 63:1

BROKEN CISTERNS

A good portion of David's life was spent on the move. He guided flocks, fled from Saul, and led troops into battle. David knew that a part of leading well was making sure his men had water. There were no rest stops or drinking fountains available. If they strayed too far from water they could die. Water was life—it was that simple. And this is the metaphor that David chose for God. He knew physical thirst and understood that it translated directly to a thirst that was far more important.

In Jeremiah 2:13 we see that God is not the only place we as sinful people turn in our attempts to slake our souls' thirst: "My people have committed two sins: They have forsaken me, the spring of living water, and have dug their own cisterns, broken cisterns that cannot hold water."

St. Augustine prayed in his *Confessions*, "You have made us for yourself, O Lord, and our hearts are restless until they find their rest in you." We know that restlessness often fills our hearts. In response, we frequently seek to satisfy our longings apart from God. We may be consumed with doing things *for* God, but even our motives for doing good are often angled away from God. Our desires are twisted and turned elsewhere. The purpose of this exercise is to search our hearts to see what really does consume us. What fills our emptiness; what satisfies our longings and our thirst? Do our souls truly thirst for God? Is it really Him we long for? Are we pursuing broken wells, or the fountain of living water?

In order to understand how and to what our thirst drives us, we must first evaluate what our soul, mind, and body are pursuing. We must honestly ask the Holy Spirit to help us see the direction we are actually headed, not just where we think we are going. The journey toward life involves walking away from the cisterns we have dug in our hope of finding satisfaction, and returning again and again to God Himself, the spring of fresh, unpolluted living water.

The questions that follow are designed to be completed now and considered again many times in the future. Bringing your true self into the light for examination by the Spirit is an aspect of self-reflection and honesty that is imperative to your spiritual journey. Dawson Trotman, founder of the Navigators, held the conviction that we reproduce after our own kind. The question then follows, "What am I spiritually reproducing?" As we mentor others, we want the reproduction of our own spiritual life to be as true to the character of Christ as possible, as much as it is within our power to make it so. As we look into the Lord's face, the Holy Spirit transforms us into that same image (2 Corinthians 3:18). If we are to invite others to imitate us as we imitate Him, then we must examine our lives for anything that does not reflect Him. "Do not conform to the pattern of this world, but be transformed by the renewing of your mind. Then you will be able to test and approve what God's will is—his good, pleasing and perfect will" (Romans 12:2). This process of spiritual transformation is one that will take conscious choice to maintain throughout your life.

Paul speaks of this evaluation in I Corinthians 3:10-15. Using the metaphor of a building, he reminds his readers that each person's works will be tested for their true value:

> But each one should build with care. For no one can lay any foundation other than the one already laid, which is Jesus Christ. If anyone builds on this foundation using gold, silver, costly stones, wood, hay or straw, their work will be shown for what it is, because the Day will bring it to light. It will be revealed with fire, and the fire will test the quality of each person's work. If what has been built survives, the builder will receive a reward. If it is burned up, the builder will suffer loss but yet will be saved—even though only as one escaping through the flames.

If this is true, then we must ask whether we are currently using our time and talents to build the Kingdom of heaven or to construct and protect our own small kingdoms. If you consider this question deliberately over time with a willing heart, the Holy Spirit will be faithful to show you the answer.

According to II Corinthians 13:5, our openness to the Holy Spirit's work is revealed by this work of self-reflection:

> Examine and test and evaluate your own selves to see whether you are holding to your faith and showing the proper fruits of it. Test and prove yourselves [not Christ]. Do you not yourselves realize and know [thoroughly by an ever-increasing experience] that Jesus Christ is in you—unless you are [counterfeits] disapproved on trial and rejected? (AMP)

Sanctification is an arduous process, not a one-time event. As Dallas Willard says, "Grace is not opposed to effort, it is opposed to earning." In the work of self-evaluation, we undertake a partnership with the Holy Spirit which will lead us to a fuller awareness and expression of the mirror piece that God has intended for us to reflect to the world.

Progession #5: Personal Inventory

Pray with David: "Search me, O God, and know my heart; test me and know my anxious thoughts. See if there is any offensive way in me, and lead me in the way everlasting" (Psalm 139:23, 24).

Prayerfully consider your life in light of the following questions, and record your responses in dialogue with God. Write this as an interaction in God Story format. If you find this especially difficult, you might prayerfully answer the questions first and then converse with God about your answers. Consider each item in both the present and the past tense.

1) Look at your life. How do you spend your time, money, and energy?

2) What do you emphasize as important to your children? Ask them to honestly reflect this back to you. What do you value for them? What do you push them toward? Again, ask them for honest feedback. If they need to think about it, don't rush them.

3) What life focus would your husband/wife, family members, roommates, co-workers, and friends say you have? Ask them to help you take an honest look.

4) What do you avoid?

5) What do you do when you are bored or lonely?

6) What makes you angry? What about these things makes you angry? What frustrated goal, purpose or direction does your anger reflect?

7) What do your life choices say about what you believe will satisfy the deep longings of your heart?

8) What are the broken wells you pursue?

Chapter 10
Adjusting the Course

"Stand in shock, heavens, at what you see!
Throw up your hands in disbelief—this can't be!"
God's Decree
"My people have committed a compound sin:
they've walked out on me, the fountain
Of fresh flowing waters, and then dug cisterns—
cisterns that leak, cisterns that are no better than sieves.
Jeremiah 2:12-13 (The Message)

TWO SINS

As we live life outside the garden, away from the face-to-face intimacy with God that we were created for, we will keenly feel our thirst. In Psalm 63, David writes, "O God, You are my God, earnestly will I seek You; my inner self thirsts for You, my flesh longs and is faint for You, in a dry and weary land where no water is" (AMP). The sons of Korah choose the same metaphor: "As the hart pants and longs for the water brooks, so I pant and long for You, O God. My inner self thirsts for God, for the living God. When shall I come and behold the face of God?" (Psalm 42:1-2 AMP).

And yet Jeremiah's indictment speaks to how we have rebelled, committing two sins. First, we have forsaken God. And like Eve, we have taken it upon ourselves to make sure our thirst gets satisfied. The word picture is clear: we have walked away from the bubbling spring pushing up from the ground unbidden in order to create our own holding tanks for water we hope to find elsewhere.

Our sincerest beliefs are not measured by the words we say but by the way we choose to live our lives. If this is true, then what does our pursuit of broken, leaky cisterns have to do with our ability to hear God? If I am heading in my own direction looking for what satisfies my soul, then I am clearly telling God that I do not think He can quench my soul's thirst. I clearly do not trust Him to provide what He created my heart to long for. A.W. Tozer says that God is always speaking to us. If we do not hear Him, it is because we are not tuned to the right frequency. What frequencies, then, are my ears, my eyes, my heart, my mind tuned to? What do I allow to occupy and influence my attentions? *What do I spend my life on?*

Missing the Point

This search for satisfaction apart from God can be most difficult to see in religious settings, where right answers are abundant. The words of truth may be there, but the motivation for our actions and the resulting fruit can be hard to discern. However, the difficulty of this important pursuit does not mean that we should abandon it. Jesus speaks to the emptiness of mere religious activity in Matthew's gospel, saying, "Not everyone who says to me, 'Lord, Lord,' will enter the kingdom of heaven, but only the one who does the will of my Father who is in heaven. Many will say to me on that day, 'Lord, Lord,' did we not prophesy in your name, and in your name drive out demons and in your name perform many miracles?' Then I will tell them plainly, 'I never knew you. Away from me, you evildoers!'" (Matthew 7:21-23).

The dictionary defines "Lord" as someone having power, authority or influence. So in my life, who has that control? What are the ways that I am saying "Lord, Lord" but have not submitted to the terrifying reality of not being the one who is in control? Am I missing the point altogether?

Eugene Peterson's rendering of Jesus' words in The Message sheds a slightly different light on Jesus' words:

> Knowing the correct password—saying 'Master, Master,' for instance— isn't going to get you anywhere with me. What is required is serious obedience—doing what my Father wills. I can see it now—at the Final Judgment thousands strutting up to me and saying, 'Master, we preached the Message, we bashed the demons, our God-sponsored projects had everyone talking.' And do you know what I am going to say? 'You missed the boat. All you did was use me to make yourselves important. You don't impress me one bit. You're out of here.' (Matthew 7:21-23 The Message)

We live in a culture that loves answers which keep life manageable, feeding on status and good impressions. As inhabitants of this broken world, we run the risk of unwittingly transferring our misinformed understanding onto God by trying to impress Him even as He refuses to meet us on these worldly terms. But you might say, "I am not doing that. I am a committed Christian; I am active in serving God." Are you sure? Have you asked God to speak to you about this? We must bow our knee to Him on His terms.

Motivations of the Heart

Sin is, at the core, a matter of the heart. Sin is not merely a matter of actions done or left undone. Before God, my life will be measured by its direction, not merely by the things I do. It may be helpful, in discerning my direction, to imagine God on one end of a continuum and all the things that provide me with life at the other. Are you consistently moving toward God, or toward these other sources of life? The direction we take will reflect our sinful patterns to find life on our own apart from God. On the outside the cup may be clean, but inside, it may be full of self-centered motives.

Consider the directional nature of the following verses:

- "My people have… walked out on Me." (Jeremiah 2:13 The Message)
- "My people have been lost sheep; their shepherds have led them astray and caused them to roam on the mountains. They wandered over mountain and hill and forgot their own resting place." (Jeremiah 50:6)
- "…Turning away from following our God." (Isaiah 59:13 AMP)
- "We all, like sheep, have gone astray, each of us has turned to our own way." (Isaiah 53:6)

Through Jeremiah we hear God's invitation, "You will seek me and find me when you seek me with all your heart" (Jeremiah 29:13). God desires that we seek after Him with our whole hearts—with the entirety of our very being. Where *is* your heart? Consider the themes that emerged from journaling through the *Personal Inventory* in Progression #5. Psalm 1 calls the person "blessed" that does not walk in the counsel of the ungodly, nor stand in the way with sinners, nor sit in the seat of those who scorn the things of God. All these actions are movements toward broken cisterns, sources of life that are not from God.

In Hosea 6:1, the Israelites cry, "Come, let us return to the Lord." But from the verses that follow, we see that God is not impressed with their words. He wants the hearts of His people, and He sees that their hearts and words do not match. The book of Hosea is one of the most sorrowful and revealing books of the Bible as the heart of Israel's faithful Husband is laid out for the entire world to see.

God does a strange thing in the book of Hosea. Hosea is a young prophet, a man known for his purity and undefiled way of life; a young man committed to preventing anything unholy from entering the gateways of his eyes, his ears, or his mouth; his hands have never touched a thing that is not holy to the Lord. This is a young man passionate for the holiness of God. God instructs Hosea to take a prostitute for a wife. What could God possibly be thinking? Hosea must be mortified, uncertain if this could possibly be the voice of God. Hosea knows well the *voice* of God, but this instruction must seem almost beyond comprehension, beyond reason itself. However, Hosea does what God asks him to do, in complete obedience. In obedience he marries the prostitute Gomer, and in so doing he touches the *heart* of God. Through the marriage relationship that follows, Hosea experiences and intimately knows the *sorrow* of God. For him to be able to plumb the depths of what Israel's harlotry is like for God, he must tangibly experience these for himself. It is impossible to understand God's heart vicariously or from a distance. Hosea experiences firsthand the pain of a wife who runs after other lovers. Because of Hosea's obedience, we are offered a window into God's heart that we would not have seen otherwise.

In Hosea, the metaphor used to reflect the idea of broken wells is that of other lovers:

> Therefore, behold, I [the Lord God] will hedge up her way [even yours, O Israel] with thorns; and I will build a wall against her that she shall not find her paths. And she shall follow after her lovers but she shall not overtake them; and she shall seek them [inquiring for and requiring them], but shall not find them. Then shall she say, Let me go and return to my first husband, for then was it better with me than now. For she has not noticed, understood, or realized that it was I [the Lord God] Who gave her the grain and the new wine and the fresh oil, and Who lavished upon her silver and gold which they used for Baal and made into **his image**.
>
> And I will visit [punishment] upon her for the feast days of the Baals, when she burned incense to them and decked herself with her earrings and nose rings and her jewelry and went after her lovers and *forgot Me, says the Lord.* **Therefore, behold, I will allure her [Israel] and bring her into the wilderness, and I will speak tenderly and to her heart.** There I will give her her vineyards and make the Valley of Achor [troubling] to be for her a door of hope and expectation. And she shall sing there and respond as in the days of her youth and as at the time when she came up out of the land of Egypt. And it shall be in that day, says the Lord, that you will call Me **Ishi [my Husband]**, and you shall no more call Me **Baali [my Baal].** For I will take away the names of Baalim [the Baals] out of her mouth, and they shall no more be mentioned or seriously remembered by their name.

And I will betroth you to Me forever; yes, *I will betroth you to Me in righteousness and justice, in steadfast love, and in mercy.* I will even betroth you to Me in *stability and in faithfulness*, and **you shall know** (recognize, be acquainted with, appreciate, give heed to, and cherish) **the Lord**.
And I will sow her **for Myself** anew in the land, and I will have love, pity, and mercy for her who had not obtained love, pity, and mercy; and I will say to those who were not My people, *You are My people*, and they shall say, ***You are my God!*** (Hosea 2:6-8,13-17,19-20,23 AMP—italics and bold lettering mine)

Progession #6: Your Chosen Direction
As you go back and re-read this, journal through the words with the assumption that they are written specifically about you. Indeed, these words are to you and to me. What is going on in your heart as you read them? Spend time in written conversation with God about what you have just read.

Hosea longed to have his wife love him, cling to him, and be loyal to him. He sought after her, he bought her back off the slave block when her lovers were finished with her and sold her. He was there to draw her off alone and apart where he could speak tenderly to her heart. His longing was the same as God's longing: "You will call me ISHI (husband)."

We cannot love Baal and our true husband (Ishi). We cannot love the things of the world and Ishi. We cannot give our lives for both perishing and eternal treasures.

> Abba, I know at times I look for something new: what I can eat, look at, or buy? I have noticed that there is a restlessness in my soul that has become a reason to shop or to anticipate a favorite food. If I allow those things to touch the restlessness, I am distracted. Lord, what if I did not distract? What if I allowed myself to feel the restlessness—invited You to examine it, allowed it to be my invitation to visit with You? In John 4, the woman at the well did not know of the depth of her thirst; but You did, and You drew attention to it. **Yes, My dear child, if you knew where the restlessness in your heart comes from – if you identified it as the same thirst I wanted to satisfy for her – you would ask Me and I would touch it as I did her thirst with an awareness of Myself and what I offer. Your thirst is My opportunity to connect to you. I would give you water you know not of and you would never thirst again. Instead, you would experience this restlessness you so fear as a desire for Me and you would run to Me, the Fountain of Living Water. Haven't you heard My voice? "Ho, you who are thirsty, come and drink..."** Lord, none of the things that distract from my restlessness/thirst are bad in and of themselves, but when I let my restlessness linger on one of them and find a reprieve then I am sating my thirst with something other than You. How sad for both of us. I mistake the sound of Your voice for something else, something I can control.

Change direction, child! What is it I am more committed to avoiding than I am committed to seeking You, Jesus? **Living in the ordinary, child, being still with Me, not on task, accomplishing. Only a few things are necessary, no, only 'one thing' is necessary. Choose with Mary. Choose with Joshua. Choose with Daniel. Choose with Paul.** This 'one thing' I do, I press toward the mark of the high calling of God in Christ Jesus. (Philippians 3:13)
"For my determined purpose is that I may know You, that I may progressively become more deeply and intimately acquainted with You, perceiving and recognizing and understanding the wonders of Your Person that I may in that same way come to know the power outflowing from Your resurrection which it exerts over believers and that I may so share Your sufferings as to be continually transformed in spirit into Your likeness, even to Your death." (Philippians 3:10)

Chapter 11
The Road Home

**"A new command I give you: Love one another.
As I have loved you, so you must love one another.
By this everyone will know that you are my disciples,
if you love one another."
John 13:34, 35**

A RELATIONAL ENQUIRY

Up to this point, our focus has been primarily set on our relationship with God. We will now turn our eyes to the horizontal plane of human relationship. Even this is "God-focused," because our relationships with people reflect either our relationship with God or our lack thereof.

Because mentoring is about relationships, we must take a close look at how we have handled and are handling our relationships with all those God has placed in our lives. We are imparting not a formula, but our very lives to others. Because we are sinful, we have sinful patterns of relating of which we are not even aware. This exercise is designed to bring those patterns to light. Then, as we mentor, we can bring these habits of heart before the Lord in prayer and keep our eyes open for them. We do not want to do anything to cause a brother or sister in Christ to stumble or to be confused or discouraged.

Turn your eyes to how well you reflect Jesus Christ in loving those around you. What is the good you see as a pattern in your life? What are the sinful relational patterns that you will want to take before Him to be changed? Philippians 2 tells us that we should have the mind of Christ toward one another. We want to strengthen the patterns in our lives where that is true. We also want to root out, cast off, and build anew the patterns that do not yet reflect Him.

Wake Up!

In Revelation 3:1-3, Jesus addresses the church in Sardis:

> ...You are supposed to be alive, but [in reality] you are dead. Rouse yourselves and keep awake, and strengthen and invigorate what remains and is on the point of dying; for I have not found a thing that you have done [any work of yours] meeting the requirements of My God or perfect in His sight. So call to mind the lessons you received and heard; continually lay them to heart an obey them, and repent. In

> case you will not rouse yourselves and keep awake and watch, I will come upon you like a thief, and you will not know or suspect at what hour I will come. (AMP)

And then again the church in Laodicea:

> I know your [record of] works and what you are doing; you are neither cold nor hot. Would that you were cold or hot! So, because you are lukewarm and neither cold nor hot, I will spew you out of My mouth! For you say, I am rich; I have prospered and grown wealthy, and I am in need of nothing; and you do not realize and understand that you are wretched, pitiable, poor, blind, and naked. (Revelation 3:15-17 AMP)

We are a spiritually impoverished people. We have set the values and the gods of this world before our eyes and have been lulled to sleep. But next, Jesus speaks to us, His church:

"Behold, I stand at the door and knock; if anyone hears and listens to and heeds My voice and opens the door, I will come in to him and eat with him, and he [will eat] with Me" (Revelation 3:20 AMP). Now, eating together was the most intimate interaction in Hebrew culture outside of the marriage bed. Beloved, if there is a wall between you and Jesus, you must forsake all in order to experience intimate relationship with Him, to hear His voice. Abandon your life that you might find it. The bridge to spiritual depth is in recognizing what is really blocking our relationship with Jesus. We must call sin what Jesus calls sin.

In some circles, a great deal of time is spent explaining why Jesus could not have meant what He said. To do so blasphemes the character of God. However, when our lives do not match up with what Jesus says, we practice our own form of blasphemy. Years ago, when my three sons still lived at home, I kept my office in the house so that I was available should they need me. One evening when I finished counseling, I came into the kitchen and at some point behaved badly toward my sons. One of them asked, "Mom, how can you go into your office and tell people how to live their lives according to the plumb line of the Word of God and then come out here and behave like this?" How indeed? A double-minded man is unstable in all his ways. Could those who know you ask the same question? What would your answer be? God is inviting us to speak truth in our inmost being, for He requires truth in the inner man—if we would hear His voice and know Him intimately, we must change our course and not just adjust our behaviors.

Progession #7: Relationship Inventory

1. Read back through Revelation 3. Record what God is saying to you and respond to Him in writing.

2. Write through the following instructions and questions. The purpose of this enquiry is to take stock of the direction in which your life is moving. This is an opportunity to turn and repent of any direction in which you detect movement toward false sources of life. Ponder long, and continue the dialogue you have begun with God using these points to provoke thoughtful conversation. Journal what God shows you as you think and pray through these ideas. Look for patterns of relational interaction, character clues, and personal insights. You may wish to invite a friend or family member to help you consider these:

- Make a list of all the significant relationships you have had in your life.
- Amongst these relationships, look for patterns of interaction.
- Look for patterns of dealing with relationship that might cause someone you are helping to stumble.
- Of this list of relationships, make two more lists: a) all the relationships that have endured, and b) all the relationships that are broken or where contact has been lost.
- In the relationships that have endured, what did you contribute? What did the other person bring?
- In the relationships that have ended, what went wrong? What was your part in the dissolution of the relationship? What was the other person's part?
- Considering all these relationships, interact with God about the following:

  -How close do my relationships tend to be?
  -How much or how little intimacy have I experienced in my relationships?
  -What has been the purpose and intent of my heart in each relationship?
  -What fears spill over into my relationships?
  -What are my expectations and demands (subtle or otherwise)?
- Examine how your relational style carries over into your relationship with God.

Chapter 12
Field Guide for Leaders

I rejoiced with those who said to me,
"Let us go to the house of the Lord."
Our feet are standing in your gates, Jerusalem.
Psalm 122:1-2

ON LEADING A MENTOR TRAINING GROUP

The facilitator of a *Learning to Love the Master* group is someone who will, by his or her careful guidance and prayerful involvement, help people toward spiritual growth and the ability to mentor others. This role is an important one which will require additional time investment and a willingness to clearly communicate and uphold expectations of the cohort, as well as keeping everyone up to date with basic logistics. Following are specific instructions for establishing and beginning a *Learning to Love the Master* mentor training group.

Before the First Session

1. **Interview Potential Members**

Take time to interview each person who is interested in participating. During this interview, give each person a detailed explanation of what is involved and required. Ask if they are willing and able to commit to being fully engaged in all group sessions, additional follow-up meetings with you, prayer partnering, praying aloud in a group, Scripture memory, extensive journaling, and transparent sharing with the group throughout the duration of the journey. Also make clear that this process is designed to encourage, strengthen, and provide direction for *persons who already have the life experiences to qualify them as a mentor.* Although the facilitator and the prayer partner will provide some elements of a mentor, the purpose of this group is not to provide mentorship. The group, rather, creates mentors by providing participants with tools for the wise handling of Scripture, an awareness of God's intimate pursuit in their own lives, and a recognition of the truths He has revealed to them in unique ways.

Some will want to join the group who do not feel at this time that God is asking them to be a mentor. Perhaps they have heard about the journey and want to "learn to love the Master" as well. Whether you allow them to join the group or not is at your discretion as the facilitator. Be very discerning as to whether this individual is ready to share his or her life at a deep level and to maintain a nonjudgmental spirit as he/she listens to others tell their stories. If a person is not yet ready to be a mentor or cannot commit to the rigorous year-long requirements but still desires the experience of writing his or her God Story, consider recommending that they attend a *Learning to Love the Master* Retreat instead. Instructions for running such a retreat are included later in this chapter.

2. **Memorize the Training Verses**

As you head toward your first group meeting, commit time to memorizing the following verses in the Bible translation of your choice:

Romans 10:17
Revelation 1:3
Acts 17:11
Psalm 119:9, 11
Psalm 1:2-3

These will be important in teaching the "hand illustration" and continuing to communicate the value of holding Scripture rightly as a mentor. More on this later! As you commit these verses to memory, consider how God has used Scripture memory in your life thus far. These experiences are yours to share in the group and in follow-up meetings to encourage participants on their journey.

> Of all the tools for personal growth in Christ, scripture memory has been the most powerful in my life; the language of the Holy Spirit of God washes over my mind and transforms my thinking. When I have strayed, it has been the Holy Spirit using the Word hidden in my heart to convict me and bring me back.

3. **Assign Journey Companions**

Once the cohort is determined, prayerfully consider the assignment of prayer partners. These journey companion pairs will review verses and pray together for 30 minutes each week. They will also hold one another accountable to consistent keeping of the Devotional Journal and regular time spent writing the God Story Journal. Much prayer should go into the assigning of prayer partners. You will probably find that you will pair and re-pair different people before you finally feel peace about all your choices. Do not make the assignments until you feel right about your decisions: these individuals will be linked together for at least a year, with the potential for lasting involvement in each other's lives. This is an opportunity for those who have never before had a prayer partner to experience the beauty of this unique and valuable relationship.

Guidelines for Pairing Journey Companions

- Splitting up good friends is usually best. The tendency among friends is to avoid the relational cost of accountability and to allow each other to sidestep requirements. The friendship is often more important than the friend, so to speak.
- Try to assign partners who have similar life situations. Pastors' wives, people with similar struggles, or people with similar schedules can be well suited to encourage each other.
- Look for people with complimentary strengths. There may be someone who can offer a needed strength to another's weakness and receive from the other's gifting in an area of their own weakness.
- Take natural temperaments into account. You may wish to put strong personalities together so they don't overwhelm a more tentative soul.

4. **Set Up Your Notebook**

At the beginning of the journey, designate a page in your notebook for each person. Include their life/year verses, birth date, address, and phone number. When each person shares, go to his or her page and jot pertinent notes about their story. This helps you pray for the individual and serves as a springboard for Guidepost appointments. Guideposts are individual follow-up times you will have with each person to interact in a way which does not happen in the group sessions.

4. **Arrange Guidepost Appointments**

As the Pilgrims' Guide, you will meet one-on-one with each group member for a 45-60 minute block on a regular and rotating basis. If you have four in your group, you would conceivably meet with each person once a month. If you have eight you will meet with each sojourner once every two months. What has worked best for me is to bring a sack lunch and meet with a couple of people in consecutive time slots on the same day. If one of you has children who need to be supervised, you can meet at a park or at a fast food restaurant with a playground. Arrange these meetings in whatever way works best for both of you.

Just as a guidepost on a physical pilgrimage provides an opportunity to gain a sense of place and to designate future direction, Guidepost appointments give you a chance to help each person recognize his or her current spiritual geography and clarify direction for the next leg of their journey. During Guidepost appointments, you will want to follow up on anything you have noted on the participant's personal page in your notebook. If time permits, you may wish to check in with him or her on how some element in their journey is going, whether it be the Devotional Journal, the God Story Journal, Scripture memory, or weekly times with their Journey Companion. The aim of this sort of check-in is not to correct behavior so much as to discuss the motivations of the heart and the beliefs about God which underlie emerging choices and patterns. Take notes on any pertinent information that arises during these appointments so you can continue to hold the person accountable and encourage them during future interactions.

***Learning to Love the Master* Group Format:**

Cohorts should be limited to a maximum of eight sojourners, although four to six is ideal. A two-hour block of time for group meetings is preferable. Groups may meet either on a weekly or a bi-monthly basis. The frequency of meetings will affect the intensity of the workload. Participants may find it easier to make time to write within a two-week rhythm. However, the weekly meetings provide a greater sense of momentum and focus. Do what works best for your group.

This journey requires a high level of commitment. No one should join after the second session unless you, as a leader, are willing to spend extra time outside of the meeting covering all the introductory material. No one should enter after the third session. All members are expected to commit for the entire duration of the group. Motivation for the journey will come from you as a facilitator and from reading and discussing the materials during the first sessions.

The format is user friendly, open-ended, and subject to the discretion of the leader. Be familiar with all the parts of the Guidebook so that you can be sensitive to any situation in which it is wise to re-read a particular part of the introduction or one of the teaching sections according to the needs of your group. The format for the first three sessions is a general guideline, so please feel free to adjust whatever you feel necessary.

Praying in the Round

Each session should begin and end with a time of praying aloud where each person participates in turn. Ask the person to your left or right to begin, and after everyone else in the circle has prayed in order, close in prayer. Praying aloud in this manner eliminates long pauses and invites each sojourner to personally engage with God during the session, dedicating the time for His purposes. It should be given priority even if some present feel uncomfortable praying aloud.

Session One:

Group members should already have read Chapter 1.
Each person should come with their notebook, Bible, and any writing utensils they will normally use for journaling.

- Be firm about starting and ending on time.
- Have students introduce themselves.
- Pray in the Round. Begin praying on time even if only one or two have arrived.
- Explain the purpose of this pilgrimage and the desired outcome. Impart the vision!
- Read and discuss the *Itinerary* from Chapter 2.
- Read and commit to the *Cohort Promise* together.
- Choose a way to read through the Chapter 2 section on *Devotional Journaling*: select a volunteer to read it aloud or assign sections and have people take turns reading it to the group. Discuss the Devotional Journaling process.
- Read *Setting Out* (Chapter 2) as a group. Allow each person to read through the *Psalm 139* questions and reflections silently. Give group members thirty minutes to practice Devotional Journaling based on this passage. Afterwards, have each person share what he or she wrote.
- Give assignments. Before the next session sojourners should:
  -Practice Devotional Journaling on a daily basis, choosing a book of the Bible to begin reading and interacting with God about in writing.
  -Read Chapter 3.
  -Come to the next meeting prepared to read from their Devotional Journal.

Session Two:

- Have everyone share from his or her Devotional Journal.
- Present the *Hand Illustration*. There is an explanation of how to do this at the end of this section. You should have the verses for the *Hand Illustration* memorized and be able to give the illustration fluidly. This helps support the Bible reading and memorization required in this course.
- Read the *Scripture Memory* section from Chapter 2 aloud. Hand out the Topical Memory System. Go over the contents. Assign two verses per week following the outline given in the Topical Memory System. If possible, share your own personal experience regarding the benefit of scripture memory.

- Give assignments. Before the next session, Group members should:
  -Continue the daily practice of Devotional Journaling.
  -Memorize the first two verses, along with topic and reference.
  -Read Chapter 4.

Session Three:

- Have everyone share from his or her Devotional Journal.
- Review verses together.
- Assign Journey Companions. Discuss weekly verse review, prayer, and accountability.
- Read and discuss the *Overview* of the God Story Journal in Chapter 6.
- Discuss the open-ended time frame for each person's God Story Journal. There is no time limit on the writing Progressions; each person may take as long as they need. If a sojourner has no more to add to a particular Progression, he or she may move on to the next one. Group members may always write and share more on any previous Progression if God gives them new information. Going back is always encouraged.
- Give assignments. Before the next session, Group members should:
  -Continue the daily practice of Devotional Journaling.
  -Memorize the third and fourth verses, along with topic and reference.
  -Meet with their respective Journey Companions in person or by phone for prayer, Scripture memory review, and accountability.
  -Begin writing their God Story journal, starting with Progression #1.
  -Read Chapter 5.

Future Sessions:

- Always be firm about starting and ending on time.
- Start by Praying in the Round.
- At least once a month, check in with group members to see how Scripture memory is going.
- Jump right in to the reading of God Stories, and continue until the time for closing prayer arrives. If you do not make it through each person's reading, make note of who still needs to share and pick up there at the next session.
- End in time to close by Praying in the Round.

Facilitating the Sharing of God Stories

Remember that story sharing is NOT a discussion. You will need to guard carefully that cohort members do not give advice or start teaching in response to what a person shares from their journal. Rather, the time of listening should be recognized as a holy moment in which we are given the opportunity to gaze upon God in the lives of others and share our story about God's presence in our lives.

After a group member has finished sharing, the best response is, "Thank you very much for sharing. What do you need from us?" A person might ask for prayer. Some have said, "I needed you to listen, and you have done just that." Others may want to look into each person's eyes to acknowledge the moment. After a person has shared and you have offered what they have requested in response, have the person on their left pray for them if they have not already requested prayer. If a person has shared something particularly difficult or if the person is clearly distressed, have several group members lay hands on the person and pray for them.

The next question is, "Who would like to share next?" Resist the temptation to edit the person's story or ask questions. Our job at this point is to listen. Make sure that this is clear to all fellow sojourners. It will feel awkward not to give feedback or say something to reassure the person, but that is not necessary. If you do so, it will certainly take away from the purpose of the time together. Any observations or questions that you have as a facilitator should be noted on that sojourner's specific page in your notebook. If you have a concern, you can bring it up during your individual Guidepost appointment with that person or give them a call at some point.

If possible, have a wise and godly counselor or mentor in mind should someone in your group encounter issues which require insight or experience beyond where you as a leader feel comfortable helping them. It is possible that the process of remembering will bring to the surface traumatic experiences which a participant has long denied, completely forgotten, or simply never shared with anyone. While the purposes of this group do not entail counseling or soul-care, such resources may be a healing next step.

Occasionally you will have a person who shares too long. To avoid discouragement and fatigue in the larger group, ask that no one share longer than 20 minutes at a time. Don't be rigid, though. The time shared by each individual will vary from week to week. Be sure all the members have shared before anyone shares for a second time, that all have shared for a second time before anyone shares for a third time, etc. Remember that you are learning about God the Father, the Holy Spirit, and Jesus Christ as you are being invited to share each individual's relationship with Him. This is where your vision of who God is will begin to expand. Relax.

God is in control of this.

Each person will travel through the material at a different pace. Some may even go back to previous Progressions as God brings new memories. The material and format is well suited to each person being in a different place, because discussion is not required.

On Scripture Memory

Even though the sojourners will be reviewing scripture memory with their journey companions, if a twosome does not have one committed person, they can both slide; no one is held accountable, and verses don't get memorized. At least monthly, go around the group and ask each participant where he/she is and what struggles he/she might be having. If someone is struggling, call him/her to encourage them and hear their verses for a few weeks to give them a boost.

This is one of the few things that is a requirement for this journey. Your mindset must be that this is not an option, and you need to be faithful to it yourself. If this is hard for you, ask one of the committed people in the cohort to hold you accountable.

This assignment will receive the most resistance—probably because it is one of the most profoundly transforming aspects of this particular pilgrimage. Satan will fight you on this one. Stand firm.

THE HAND ILLUSTRATION

Use the Hand Illustration to introduce Scripture memory. The human hand gives us an excellent picture of a balanced mastery of the Word of God in our lives. As the degree of difficulty increases in our apprehension of the Word of God, so does resistance from the enemy. We want to help one another all we can to be balanced Christians using wisely the Word of God.

For the word of God is living and active. Sharper than any double-edged sword,
it penetrates even to dividing soul and spirit, joints and marrow;
it judges the thoughts and attitudes of the heart. (Hebrews 4:12)

Ephesians 6:10-17 describes the battle gear of the believer and the enemy of the believer. The Word of God is referred to as the Sword of the Spirit. As believers, we want to handle well this offensive and defensive weapon, which has been given to us by the Spirit of God.

So what is involved in mastering this Sword which belongs to the Holy Spirit?

Pick up your Bible. Identify it as the Sword of the Spirit. Talk about its characteristics as you describe the importance of each finger in grasping and wielding it. Be sure that you quote the appropriate verse with each finger.

Now begin to work your way through the fingers of the hand, beginning with the little finger. Try to pick up the Bible with your little finger alone (Hearing). Can you use it? Is the enemy threatened? Can the Holy Spirit help you if you cannot even pick up His Sword?

Now move to the ring finger (Reading), and pick up the Bible with it and the little finger. How much trouble will Satan have taking the Sword from your hand? Can you use it effectively for offense or defense?

Next move to the middle finger (Study). Pick up your Bible, and wield it as a sword. Are you better able to use it effectively in offensive as well as defensive ways?

Next is the index finger (Memorization). Pick up your Bible, and wield it as a sword. Try to pull it from your hand with your other hand, or ask someone in the class to try to get it from you. Allow them to do so, but put some struggle into it.

Finally, move to the thumb (Meditation). Grasp the Bible firmly with your whole hand, and ask someone in the cohort to try to get it away from you now. Hold on for dear life.

Brandish that Bible. You want to make the point that when all five methods of taking in the Word of God are in place, you are well able to take over the turf of the enemy, and you are able to defend your own stance and that of others.

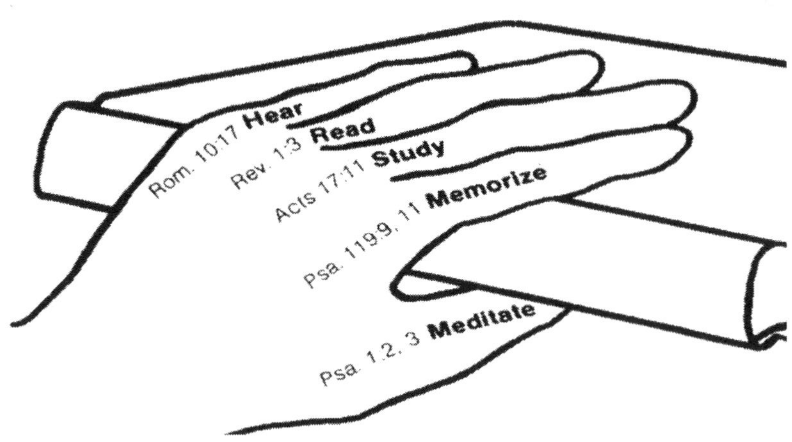

The Word Hand by The Navigators, ©1964. All rights reserved.

It is important for you as the Leader to have the verses to the individual fingers memorized.

Hearing the Word from godly pastors and teachers provides us insight into others' study of the Scriptures as well as stimulating our own appetites for the Word.

Reading the Bible gives us an overall picture of God's Word. Many find a daily reading program helpful to take them systematically through the Bible.

Studying the Scriptures leads us into personal discoveries of God's truths. Writing down these discoveries helps us organize and remember them better.

Memorizing God's Word enables us to use the Sword of the Spirit to overcome Satan and temptation, as well as to have it readily available for witnessing or helping others with a "word in season."

Meditating is likened to the thumb, for it is used in conjunction with each of the other four methods. Only as we meditate on God's Word—thinking of its meaning and application to our lives—will we discover its transforming power at work within us.

ON RUNNING A *LEARNING TO LOVE THE MASTER* RETREAT

Learning to Love the Master works well in a retreat format either as a stand-alone opportunity for spiritual and community growth or as a means of kicking off a year-long mentor-training group. Leaders should already have written a good portion of their own God Story and be prepared to share from their stories and experiences as they offer teaching, guidance, and inspiration to the retreat participants. Let the participants know ahead of time to bring a journal or loose-leaf paper. Have lined paper and red and black pens on hand.

Hospitality

The goal of the retreat weekend is to provide freedom from distraction and responsibility so that participants may fully engage with the concepts, the writing process, and each other—and in so doing, encounter God in new ways. As such, the retreat location should be adequately equipped with comfortable, clean living arrangements. I highly recommend having someone outside of the cohort who is dedicated to preparing and cleaning up after meals in service of the retreat participants and leader(s) and providing snacks and beverages between meals.

Intentional Use of Time

There is a great deal of content and relationship to experience in a Learning to Love the Master Retreat! Make the most of the time by clearly communicating in advance where and when sessions will start, and aim to start on time. The breakfast meal will be a time of teaching.

Teaching

Because Retreat participants will not have read this Guidebook, certain ideas must be presented which will give them a foundation for writing their God Stories. The *Sample Itinerary* suggests a teaching schedule. As such, leaders should study the information and illustrations present in the text ahead of time and use their own God Stories to supply supporting examples. The teaching times are an opportunity to help participants see that God, in His passionate love, has been drawing them to Himself throughout their life and that each person uniquely reflects God and has unique things to offer from his or her own created identity and unfolding story.

Future Modifications

The following Itinerary presents guidelines for an initial Retreat, with a focus on understanding and practicing Progression #1. However, future *Learning to Love the Master* Retreats can be implemented which focus on other Progressions and teach further concepts included in the Guidebook. Of primary importance, in any case, is helping participants to maintain a focus on engaging relationally with God at a heart level.

Sample Itinerary

Friday Evening

5 pm: Sojourners arrive and get settled in their rooms.

6 pm: Dinner is served. Make use of this introductory time with intentional questions and conversation around the table:

- How did you get here?
- What are you longing for this weekend?
- What do you fear as you enter this retreat?
- Tell us something about yourself. What does life hold for you these days?

7 pm: **Session One**

- Pray in the Round, see *Praying in the Round*, p. 124.
- Read and agree to the *Cohort Promise*, p. 29.
- Read a *Note from the Author*, pp. 11-12.
- Read the *Introduction* together, pp. 13-15.
- Explain the purpose of this retreat from 1 John 1:3.
  "…What we have seen and heard we proclaim to you also, so that you too may have fellowship with us; and indeed our fellowship is with the Father, and with his Son Jesus Christ."
  Describe how you have experienced this firsthand through your own experience of writing your God Story and listening to the God Stories of other people. This is an opportunity to cast vision for what people can expect as they fully engage this weekend.
- If you are facilitating a men's retreat, read and discuss what John witnessed and experienced as he led a group of men on a *Learning to Love the Master* Retreat, pp. 26-27.
- Teach *The Mirror*, p. 51.
- Teach *Distorted Mirrors*, pp. 79-80.
- Teach *The Journey Of and Into Remembering*, pp. 18-22.
- Explain how this process works: we are remembering the details of our story in order to recognize God's presence in it and to hear what He wants to say about it.
- Read *Psalm 139 Meditation*, pp. 35-37. Ask the participants to close their eyes during the reading.
- Read together the *Overview and Logistics*, pp. 71-72.
- Ask the participants to read *Eyes That See*, pp. 73-75, before breakfast.

Saturday Morning

7:30 am: Breakfast and **Session Two**

- Pray in the Round.
- As they eat, read *Preparatory Postures*, p. 75, and Progression #1: *What Have You Seen?* pp. 76-77.
- Read an excerpt from your God Story.
- Dismiss the group in silence so individuals can spend four hours of focused time to think, pray, remember, and write their God Stories. After lunch, the group will reconvene to **read** and **listen**.

1 pm: Lunch

2 pm: **Session Three**

- Pray in the Round.
- Share God Stories as described in *Facilitating the Sharing of God Stories,* pp. 127-128.

6 pm: Dinner

Saturday Evening

7 pm: **Session Four**

- Pray in the Round.
- If necessary, finish the reading of God Stories.
- Spend time in worship: sing and pray, thanking God for His lifelong pursuit and the way He has revealed Himself this weekend. The time following worship could also be used for comments and questions.

Sunday Morning

7:30 am: Breakfast and **Session Five**

- Teach *Two Voices* as they eat, pp. 63-68.
- Read an excerpt from your God Story to illustrate.
- Pray in the Round.

8:30 am: Dismiss the group for four more hours of God Story writing.

12:30 pm: Lunch

1:30 pm: **Session Six**

- Gather to read and listen.
- Pray in the Round to end the retreat.

Appendix A

Excerpts from God Stories

An Excerpt from John's God Story

Father, I would like to have a conversation with You about my life…about where You were in the moment by moment unfolding of my life story.

John, you fear that I will not speak to you.

Yes, Lord, that is true.

John, you really don't believe that I love you with an everlasting love. I want you to rest in My love for you. Resting in My love neutralizes the presence of fear.

Father, fill me with a full awareness of Your love for me. You chose my parents. What part of Your glory was reflected by them and imprinted on my soul? I wonder what they felt as they prepared to be parents. I was born into a world at war (1942).

Your mother was very fearful…a son…would he live to go to war?

Her fear was realized when I went to Vietnam in 1968 at 25 years of age.

Would You speak to me about my father? I am still haunted by the psychologist's question during Post Traumatic Stress counseling at the VA. The psychologist asked, *"What did your father think of you?"* That is a question only You can answer, Father. Would You speak to that please?

John, your father's fearful heart prevented him from speaking into your life. Your brother and sister have answers to that question.

Rose Street, Youngstown, Ohio:

One of my earliest memories was throwing sticks and stones into a Buckeye tree to knock loose the ripened nuts that were encased in a protective covering with protruding thorns. The nuts were brown and very shiny. I would do this for long periods of time. I was quite passionate about doing this; I was a little boy, but I was able to pull this off. I felt very powerful when I was successful in knocking down the Buckeyes. Where were You in this?

I was enjoying you and encouraging you and drawing attention to the passion in you.

Oh Lord, where is that passion now?

The enemy has plundered much of it.

Lord, redeem that passion, especially for Your will and for Your Kingdom.

Your father saw that passion and he entered your life by spending time showing you how to make bracelets, rings and necklaces from the Buckeyes.

I remember feeling special.

I was sitting next to you and your father, delighting in your father as he delighted in you.

Thank you for that picture, Father.

The beginning of shame:

When I was about five years old, I remember playing with three play pistols. I was throwing them into the air and catching them, at least some of the time. My mother asked me not to do it anymore, because it was dangerous. There was something that felt very powerful about throwing the guns in the air and being able to catch them. It felt good. I did not heed my mother's warning, and I tossed all three into the air at the same time. I caught two of them but the third one was made of tin and it hit me in the nose. It was very painful. My mother became very emotional and wanted to take me to the doctor. My father was angry because of my disobedience and decided that I did not need to see a doctor. The end result was a scar that looked like a backward C. I had a new awareness that something was wrong with me, and this 'brand' could be seen by everyone. I felt marked. What were Your thoughts toward me here, Lord?

Although you disobeyed, that mark on your nose is a memorial of your heart coming alive to what it means to be a man… I created you to live out of the power that raised My Son from the dead, and I created you to be passionate about that life. This was a taste of what your soul was created for… the enemy stepped in and interpreted this event for you and lied to you.

You are right. About two years later when we were living on Logan Avenue, I was playing with some boys from the neighborhood; one of them called me Seabiscuit. I became full of rage and knocked him to the ground and proceeded to pummel him. The other boys pulled me off. Lord, can we talk about this rage, not in psychological language but in the language of the soul?

John, there was a great battle raging in the unseen world for your soul. The Hater was influencing your soul that day. You have been destined for the Kingdom of light before the foundation of the world but not without being scarred by the Presence of Darkness.

I often choose to avoid being seen as a man full of passion for Your Kingdom. I have just this very moment become aware of my commitment to not being laughed at or made fun of. This prevents me from living out of my heart with passion and an awareness of Your presence. I long for the freedom to be seen as foolish and remain fully committed to Your will.

Darkness distorted your power into a symbol of dark glory, something shameful. But I meant it unto you for good, and I always have My way. Remember coming alive to joy and passion and a sense of being powerful?

O, Lord Jesus, I humble myself before You and willingly submit myself to Your Kingdom's work. I resist you, Hater of my soul. I denounce the lie that it is death to be seen as foolish and that I must avoid being laughed at. Father, I long to draw near to You and to live out Your Glory in me.

And so you shall, son.

Vietnam:

I remember the emptiness of December, 1967. I was a very fearful young man. I sensed the shallowness of my relationships. Life was moving too fast. I felt very disconnected from friends and family; life seemed very dark and hopeless. Where were You? No one discussed how they felt about the impending assignment to Vietnam. That was the pattern in my home. We didn't talk about anything, especially how we felt.

Just prior to leaving for Vietnam, my uncle Steve came unexpectedly to our home. I went out to greet him. He was a Marine veteran of the Korean War—he had been wounded. I remember his words: "Hey kid, keep your head down." He gave me a big hug and then left for work. As I look back, it was You, Father.

Yes, you needed to be encouraged, John; he was the only one available to Me, and I sent him to you.

At the airport, I remember sad faces but no words. My heart was empty, and I felt very alone. But then You showed up again. I sat next to a sergeant who was on his way to Vietnam for the 2nd time and again the words, "Kid, it's going to be ok." Lord, that had to be You again.

Yes, I was sitting next to you, son.

January, 1968: I arrived in country: "The Pond," as it was affectionately called. We trucked up country from Saigon to Ben Hoa reception center. The unit that I was assigned to was no longer functioning, and it took longer than usual to get assigned to a regular unit, which caused me a great deal of anxiety. Again, I felt lonely and out of control.

Where were You in Vietnam? There were reminders of You that began to bring my heart alive. Lt. Hall came to help us with our perimeter defensive posture after he had been wounded. Even though he was a part of a cult You still used him to get me thinking about You again. He invited me to fellowship with a group of men of his faith. I went but never returned, because the leader said I could not take communion with them. I so wanted to belong; instead, I was rejected.

John, I was there, arousing your heart and not allowing you to go down a wrong path.

Thank you, Father, for protecting me.

Lt. Hall and I became friends. A friend of his girlfriend was a teacher. She sent tapes and notes from her second- and third- grade students. It was such an encouragement to read their notes and listen to their tapes. What was Your purpose in that Lord?

John, your hard heart needed softening; you had hardened it against the uncaring world you grew up in. I chose little children to help me. I could always get close to you through children. I saw how you loved to teach the handicapped children to swim. You loved and received love in return from the children you taught.

I remember going with another officer to make a solatium payment to a Vietnamese military family. One of our personnel had accidentally killed the husband. We had to travel some very dangerous roads. It was very quiet; it felt dark and foreboding—what if I died on this road? I began to think about life after death.

John, I was opening your eyes to the spiritual realm. I was stirring your heart to seek Me as you had in your early faith as a child.

The awareness of danger and the sense of foreboding and the questions about death convinced me to attend a Mass on Good Friday. It felt empty and void of meaning. More darkness, Lord, but this time in the darkness there was a crack in my heart; I began to hope that I could find You, that I would find You.

John, that is because Patti's sister's letters spoke to you of Me. She was My voice to you in that very dark place. Although you had not yet met her she was willing to listen to My leading when I asked her to tell you about Me and My love for you and to keep telling you. Slowly, ever so slowly, I began to erode the wall of resistance that you had put up against My love.

My Darling Wife Patti:

Thank You for Patti. What a precious gift. I remember meeting her in Colorado Springs, September, 1967. You arranged for us to meet. She was faithful to talk about You and Jesus. I remember arguing about the reality of Jesus.

I presented a good gift to you John, but your heart was hard. Your excessive drinking prevented you from seeing the truth.

I lament not desiring to go to church with her that Sunday morning. She dropped by on her way to invite me; she was beautiful. I remember that morning. I was hung over and my heart was hard, and I felt ashamed. Your pursuit of me has been and continues to be relentless.

The night before leaving Colorado Springs, we went to my going away party, and I ignored her. She was just an ornament. How I damaged her heart. That night, Patti was trying very hard to please me—packing and organizing all my stuff along with my roommate Bill, while I sat in the middle of the room and sorted papers. Sometime in the early hours of the morning she crashed on the couch, declaring she was exhausted. She had planned to see me off at the airport with Bill. I said, "Well, go home, then, and go to bed." I really hurt her, and she left in tears. Lord, I was caught up in my own dark world, only aware of myself, oblivious to those around me. I remember Bill's anger toward me at the airport. I thought he was going to tear me apart limb by limb. He and his girlfriend loved Patti and felt that the way I treated her was wrong on many levels.

John, you were in the camp of the Hater. It would take many months of wearing you down before you would begin to come into the light.

Lord, would You please redeem our painful beginning. I was so preoccupied I missed Your precious gift in Patti.

John, you were a very selfish young man, allowing and at times continuing to choose to allow fear to be your master.

Father, You are right, and as a result I miss the true reality of the moment by not 'Christifying' the moment, as Nouwen refers to it. I am frantically trying to keep from being seen as the poor kid who was not loved well and as a result felt great shame which most often governed my relationships. Oh, how I missed really enjoying the relationship with Patti when we were friends in Colorado Springs. The connection with Patti was brief: October through December—57 days total. We played Bridge every night into the wee hours of the morning with Bill and his girlfriend, also named Patti, and then drug off to work with little sleep, hating ourselves, but having so much fun we were back at it the next night. And then I left for Vietnam.

Yes son, but I brought turmoil into your relationship with the girl in PA—the contrast to Patti was glaring. I was drawing you toward Me, bringing light to the dark places; your heart was hard and fearful, but I was eroding the hardness.

Excerpts from Patti's God Story

The Beginning:

Isaiah 49:1…The Lord has called me from the womb, from the body of my mother. He named my name.

Psalm 22:10…I was cast upon You from my very birth; from my mother's womb. You have been my God.

Psalm 139:13…You formed my inward parts; You knit me together in my mother's womb.

Dear Father – what do I know of my beginning? So little!

Yes, child, but I know everything. There is not one second of that time I was not hovering, guarding and protecting you. Do you remember what I said to you yesterday (Isaiah 27:2-3)? "You are a vineyard, beloved, and lovely; I sing a responsive song to you and about you. I, the Lord, am your Keeper: I water you every moment, lest anyone harm you. I guard and keep you night and day. I will rejoice over you with joy… I make no mention of your past sins… I will exult over you with singing" (Malachi 3:17).

Oh Father, I wish the humans around me had known that. They were all so alone in their individual, personal hells. My grandmother: a strange mixture of tough and tender. The only arms I ever remember. I cannot remember her holding me—at least, no one event stands out; but I remember how big and soft and puffy, like a pillow, she was, and how much I loved to snuggle into her.

Mom and Dad were living with Granny, Papa, and Uncle Dan in Butte, MT when I was born. Smells, tastes, sounds: incense from the rented apartment down the long hall by the bathroom. (I hated that smell.) Paul Harvey—we always sat down to listen to him. But I think these memories belong to First Grade when I lived there again with Granny, Papa, and Dad, when Mom went on ahead to California with Larry.

Papa's tailor shop was downstairs—down long, narrow, steep, splintery wooden stairs. Remember the time I tried to roller skate down them? I think Granny caught me in the nick of time. **With some help from Me!** Those stairs led to and from Granny's Kitchen on the 2nd floor and the modest living quarters. What I remember about that huge two-story structure is rotting chartreuse wood and red brick with peeling paint. But Granny was there. I think Granny was really the mother figure for me in my early years.

Mom did not like or want kids. Dad had one from a previous marriage, though she did not live with us, and he did not want more. And certainly not another girl, I think. Mom told me years later how angry she was with her family doctor who gave here extremely erroneous information about birth control and how naive and clueless she was, and how she wished she had never had kids.

Jeremiah 1:5 "...Before I formed you in the womb I knew you and approved of you. Before you were born, I separated and set you apart, consecrating you..."

"Nurture" is the word I find myself looking for in my story. No mention of You at all. But I can see the moments of arousal—life stirring, small tastes of water that would make me thirsty—oh, so very thirsty—for more.

Howard Street:

I was 18-months-old when we moved there. So most all my memories have to include Larry, because he was born when I was 21-months-old. How interesting, that picture of mom in her fur coat and hat holding me in front of the new house had to be when she was 5 months pregnant. There is also a picture of dad all dressed up in his suit, dress coat, and hat holding me while mom takes our picture.

There are two memories of You in that house. Perhaps more will come which I will sandwich in later. The first is in my bedroom. I am small; Mom and Dad have wallpapered my whole room. There are tin soldiers marching all over the walls, and the ceiling is covered with stars. There is a border with drums and drumsticks tying the two together. The colors are red, white and blue. Interesting that it is decorated for a boy rather than a girl. Perhaps that is why I have never been frilly. I shared a room with Larry for many years to come, and I can understand why they did not pick a doll theme.

I am in my bed; it is a bunk bed and I am in the bottom bunk. Perhaps it is when I was moved out of the crib and Larry took it over. Chairs are lined up with their back against my mattress so I will not fall onto the hardwood floor. I am in there alone. There is a window at the end of this room, which seems to be a very long, narrow room. In the window is sitting a very large male angel in a cream colored garment with big, soft, velvety wings. I am not at all afraid. In fact it seems to be quite a comfort that he is there, and I sense he is there to watch over me. Today I have in my possession a book my mother must have been reading to me about that time called *The Littlest Angel*. It was a story of a little boy who died and went to heaven and became a little angel, and the big angels all watched over him for his mommy who could not be there to take care of him. I wonder as I write this, did my mom tell me that those angels would watch over me, too? At any rate, that angel sitting on the window ledge seemed real then, and as I write this he seems just as real now. There You were again, and there is the theme of nurture, only this time it is in the context of the heavenly. Nurture has found a place, this elusive location called heaven where heavenly beings took care of You, where there were heavenly beings that would take care of me. To prove it I have my very own angel sitting on my very own window sill, just sitting there leaning against the lentil with a peaceful, loving look on his face, watching over me. His face, as far as I can remember, was not familiar to me; it was the face of a pleasant man about 30 years of age. **My child, I was right there. I used that little book to make you aware of My heaven.**

Nurture:

The ceramic shop: Mom was working there, cleaning greenware, I believe. I get to go with her. Larry must be with Granny, or he is not born yet. I do not know. No, he must be born, and I must be 3 or 4, because my hair is fairly long and it took years to grow.

I like the lady who owns the shop. She is different from my mom. We go early in the day, I know because my hair is not yet combed and it is all knots and tangles. When my mom combs it she just gets the job done – she pulls and it hurts but she doesn't seem to care much about that. It was always a battle; I am crying and pulling away, and she is angry. But this lady is different; she combs the snarls from my hair without pulling – she is very patient and gentle. She starts from the bottom and works up.

I feel special, cared for, and nurtured around this lady, a little taste of what I was created for to keep my soul alive. My lady has no children; I think she pretends I am hers. She shows me how slip is poured into the rubber molds and how it is removed and cleaned and how it is painted and fired. I have a knowledge today of how that works even thought that is my only exposure. I even remember how they tell when it is baked. Amazing – Lord, is that what happens to learning when it is offered in the context of relationship?

The next memory of You while I lived on Howard Street is the death threat experience. I was 4 or 5, and I decided to walk to Ruth's house. Ruth was my mom's friend. Of course that was not allowed, but I was impulsive and forgot the rule in the face of such a great adventure. I remember seeing the 10-year-old and the 6-year-old boys across the street. I think I may have, in my 'Anne of Green Gables' way said a bouncy "hi" to them – after all I was a big girl on a great adventure. But all of a sudden, without warning, the adventure turned to a nightmare. The boys came across the street and accused me of stealing their balloon. I did not have it but they would not believe me. They beat me up and searched me to find their balloon. They took my cowboy boots away – thinking that perhaps I had hidden the balloon in them. Not finding it, the older boy was convinced I had swallowed it. He sent his 6-year-old brother home to get a knife to cut open my stomach to retrieve their prize.

I remember awaiting the return of the younger brother with terror, knowing somehow that this boy was not bluffing. He was waiting silently with me; we were hidden in the bushes, me flat on my back covered with dirt and leaves, he sitting on my chest. Just as the 6-year-old was returning, a paperboy of about 12 came by on his bike. He saw what was happening and grabbed the boys. He demanded to know what was going on. He retrieved my boots, asked what they had done with my socks (which I always put in the toes of my boots because they slipped down and were a bother), got me up, brushed me off – helped me with my boots and took me home. We had never seen that paperboy before or after that incident – he did not deliver in our neighborhood. He was kind, gentle, loving, concerned – he was my hero for years. Perhaps he was my Angel in paperboy form. Who knows? What I do know is that he further aroused in me a longing for tenderness and kindness and again I heard the Voice that was beginning to become familiar to me.

Even the moments after returning home were pleasant memories –perhaps the only memories I have of being cared for by my mom. I had been terrified to go home. I had disobeyed, and that never set well. When I got home and the boy told my parents what had happened, my mom was overcome with kindness rather than contempt. She put me in a warm tub and bathed me and washed my hair and dressed me in my warm, cozy robe. That is the most wonderful feeling I can remember in that house. I felt like a princess, rescued from the terrible dragon by the white knight and returned to the castle where her worried parents were overcome with relief. I even sported a black eye as a badge of tribute to my great and scary adventure.

I had those long summer days with Granny. She, listening to 'soaps' and dozing and I, cutting out paper dolls so very carefully and tenderly: laying each doll in a Kleenex box bed with Kleenex blankets and pillows. Getting them up ever so carefully, dressing them, loving them, and caring for them. The feeling associated with those paper dolls is so strong; so strong I was consumed with them, obsessing over them, craving more of them. Every day, or so it seemed to me, I stole another quarter from Granny's purse and walked to the store to buy yet another book of dolls and their clothes. I painstakingly created a reality with my scissors. I was very precise. These were living beings – come to love me, their mommy. I must be very careful with all that affected them. I had a very large box full of these dolls and their carefully sorted wardrobes. Could Granny have been oblivious to the missing quarters? Money was not plentiful in that household. Or could it be that she was dozing more and more because she already had Encephalitis? I do not know.

What I know for sure about that time was the feeling in my heart. I loved those dolls and the ritual I built around their care so much it hurt. It is my first memory of the feeling I now know to be bittersweet joy, and that feeling is uniquely about my relationship, my intimacy with You, Abba. This is my *'did not our hearts burn within us'* place. The first sound of the rustle of Your garment as it passed by, and I was captured by the feeling and longed for the Romance though it would be many years before I knew anyone like You would want to romance me.

As my mind races ahead, all my experiences of nurture are in my parents absence, the baby doll, the summer of mud houses, paper dolls, no mom is present. Things on Howard were cozy, though, and warm but not nurturing – not the same as at Granny's. Wow, Abba – I just realized the significance of the word "cozy." That is what people say about my house now. It is cozy. Cozy is so nurturing to my soul. When I create beauty and the cozy atmosphere it is my way of recreating a sense of Your presence. No matter how beautiful I find other homes and locations I have stayed in, I come home to a sense of You. You, Abba, are cozy! The place we inhabit together is cozy, because You are there.

Mom is in town when I have my tonsils out – I must be 8 – Mom is at the Doctor's office when I awaken from the ether – I was very ill – she was there then. But I go home to Granny's, so mom must be working and we have moved to California and returned to Butte, and it is during the time that our house was being built. Granny and I had been saving pennies in a tea can. I think she may have been paying me for things like squeezing the color into the margarine to make it look like butter. Ugh. It was fun then; now I wonder how our hearts survived that stuff. I wanted that baby doll that seemed so real. She had real wool hair dyed light brown, blue eyes that opened and closed, moveable head and limbs, ears like a real baby, and she drank water and wet a real little diaper.

When I arrived home, Granny had the doll there for me. I was truly surprised. That was probably one of the only times in my life I have not caught on to a surprise.

Oh, what a joy. I had graduated from my precious paper dolls to an 'almost-real' baby. This was no doll. This was my first child. She still lies wrapped in my doll trunk, much the worse for Wes's wear. I was conscious of her needs day and night. I kept her by me at all times so that should she need me, I would be there. As I was 'being there' for her, somehow You were 'being there' for me. I lived in a little cocoon of love. Meeting needs in order to taste needs met. You were that cocoon. Still I did not know of Your existence, but that did not deter You from cradling me in Your arms.

Even then I was dramatic and passionate and intense. I poured every fiber of my being into what I loved. Dad called me a three-act play, which must have been true; though when he spoke those words they were with contempt. Funny, he himself loved acting and singing. We were so alike. Perhaps that is the reason for the contempt. He had so much shame and self-centered contempt; he saw himself in me and tried to kill in me what he hated in himself.

The move from Butte and from my precious Granny to Vallejo, California: what do I remember of that move? It was just dad and me. All I can remember is driving over Donner Pass in a terrible snow storm in the dead of winter. I am sure we drove straight through from Butte to Vallejo without stopping anywhere to sleep.

I have a lot of memories of that time. When we arrived, I began my second semester of first grade, and when we came back to Butte I was in the third grade. There is not one memory of You, Abba, in all of my time in Vallejo. Boy, am I glad we did not stay there. That was a disruptive time for me. I had too much freedom, too much alone time. Mom is still not around. I see her in my memory bank in two frames during that whole time, and the rest of the time I am in school or on my own. Sometimes Larry is there with me and we are alone, and sometimes I am with neighborhood kids but no parents to be seen. Sometimes I am at the shop with mom or dad.

Neighborhood kids: there You are again. Abba, I had just despaired of seeing You, and then You appear. **Of course I appear, child. I was always hovering; I never left. And it was not as easy there to touch you – I did not have your Granny to work through, but I managed.**

I no longer remember the name of the little girl; it might have been Julie (I loved that name after those days). She lived right across the alley and down one house. I love to go there. Her mom was home, the house was so cozy and she had her own room: it was so beautiful, so much love had been poured into decorating it for her. You could just feel she was special to someone. I do not remember her parents, but I probably avoided them because they were adults and I felt a great deal of shame around adults. Being in that room brings back the taste of nurture Abba. There You are again plucking my heart strings. Making sure that I remember THE SONG; that I remember THE VOICE of THE ONE Who sings THE SONG.

I remember how my heart ached when it was time to leave her home and go back to our duplex. How sterile our duplex was. It was not a home. There is no warmth there, no indication of any care given to creating a place of refuge. Just bare walls and floors and no one there. It probably felt just as drab and hopeless to my mother, as she and dad did love beauty, and created it in our house on Howard Street.

Even as I write this I do not want to go back to our duplex. I can still feel the longing to stay and be Julie. I used to pretend I was Julie and they were my parents and that was my room. I wonder if I lived there in my mind more than in reality. I have always been good at living in a fantasy world of my own making. To live in that warm loving environment – to feel those feelings which touched so deeply the core of my being?

Patti, remember the words in the verses in Ephesians that you are reviewing: "That out of My glorious riches I may strengthen you with power through My Spirit in your inner being, so that Christ may dwell in your heart through faith... to the end that you may grasp with all the saints how wide and long and high and deep is the love of Christ that surpasses knowledge… that you may be filled up to the measure of all My fullness." I was even then touching the place I planned to occupy. I was building a cozy room in your heart where you and I could live together, and you would never be alone again. I was creating a thirst that would drive you into My arms. I was drawing attention to the terrible emptiness of your soul so that when I finally revealed Myself to you, you would know it was My voice that you had been hearing all along.

Appendix B
Further Reading

Michael Card, *A Lost Sorrow: Reaching Out to God in the Lost Language of Lament* (Colorado Springs: NavPress, 2005).

Dr. Larry Crabb, *Finding God* (Grand Rapids: Zondervan, 1993).

John Eldredge and Brent Curtis, *The Sacred Romance: Drawing Closer to the Heart of God* (Nashville: Thomas Nelson, 1997).

John Eldredge, *Waking the Dead: The Glory of a Heart Fully Alive* (Nashville: Thomas Nelson, 2003).

C.S. Lewis, *Mere Christianity* (San Francisco: HarperCollins Publishers, 1952).

C.S. Lewis, *The Problem of Pain* (New York: HarperCollins Publishers, 1940/1996).

C.S. Lewis, *The Weight of Glory* (New York: William B. Eerdmans Publishing Company, 1949).

Calvin Miller, *Into the Depths of God: Where Eyes See the Invisible, Ears Hear the Inaudible, and Minds Conceive the Inconceivable* (Bloomington: Bethany House Publishers, 2001).

Calvin Miller, *The Table of Inwardness: Nurturing Our Inner Life in Christ* (Downers Grove: Inter-Varsity Press, 1984).

Charles R. Swindoll, *Intimacy with the Almighty: Encountering Christ in the Secret Places of Your Life* (Nashville: Thomas Nelson, 1996).

A.W. Tozer, *The Pursuit of God: The Human Thirst for the Divine* (Camp Hill: WingSpread Publishers, 1993).

Walter Wangerin, Jr., *Reliving the Passion* (Grand Rapids: Zondervan Publishing House, 1992).

Dallas Willard, *The Great Omission: Reclaiming Jesus' Essential Teachings on Discipleship* (New York: HarperCollins Publishers, 2006).

Made in United States
Orlando, FL
19 March 2023

31203973R00083